A HARROWSMITH GARDENER'S GUIDE

VINES

Edited by Karan Davis Cutler
Illustrations by Marta Scythes

CAMDEN
•HOUSE•

PUBLISHING

Camden House Publishing, Inc.
A division of Telemedia Communications (USA) Inc.

**Library of Congress
  Cataloging-in-Publication Data**
Vines / edited by Karan Davis Cutler; illustrations
by Marta Scythes.
      p.   cm. — (A Harrowsmith gardener's guide)
      Includes bibliographical references and index.
      ISBN 0-944475-23-X
      1. Ornamental climbing plants.   2. Climbing
      plants.   I. Cutler, Karan Davis.   II. Series.
      SB427.V56   1992
      635.9'74—dc20   91-37601
                                                 CIP

Design by Eugenie S. Delaney
Illustrations by Marta Scythes
Cover by Ron Broda

Camden House Publishing, Inc.
Ferry Road
Charlotte, Vermont 05445

First Edition

Printed in Canada by
D. W. Friesen & Sons
Altona, Manitoba

Trade distribution by
Firefly Books Ltd.
250 Sparks Avenue
Willowdale, Ontario
Canada M2H 2S4

Acknowledgments

Vines: A Harrowsmith Gardener's Guide represents, in its finished state, the commitment and cooperation of many individuals. They include designer Eugenie Delaney; artist Marta Scythes, who drew the black-and-white illustrations; cover artist Ron Broda; copy editor Sharon Smith; proofreader Faith Hanson; editorial assistant Susan Walker; typist Margo Ketchum; and typesetter Sheryl Fletcher.

Other Gardener's Guides

Ground Covers
Spring Flowers
Water Gardens
Rock Gardens
Berries

Contents

Grape vine enveloping an arbor.

Chapter One:
An Introduction to Vines

By Karan Davis Cutler

here may be something that doesn't love a wall, to paraphrase Robert Frost, but it ought not be a gardener. For a wall or a fence or a post or a wire or almost any other vertical support or surface is the natural home of the vine. Most North American ivory towers are also ivy towers, but in the main, we have either ignored or remained ignorant of the virtues of climbing plants. ✍ Gardeners in other countries are not so unmindful. They use vines with abandon: rambling along old walls, swarming around rainspouts, bestriding gateways, soaring up trees, roofing over patios and porches. The British are so smitten with climbers that any English Guernsey dawdling over a clump of crimson clover is in jeopardy of being planted with clematis 'Henryi' and transformed into a living pergola. ✍ According to garden historians, vines were among the first cultivated plants. Egyptian wall paintings from the Eighteenth Dynasty (1415 B.C.) show slaves harvesting fruit from vine-covered pergolas. Romans used twining roses, ivy and other climbers to garland and shade. The grape was a mainstay of ancient Mediterranean agriculture, so common that in the Bible it is referred to simply as "the vine."

The early gardens of western Europe lent themselves to the cultivation of vines, for most lay within walls. Rare was the estate, secular or religious, that lacked an arbor. Climbing plants are a constant of history and literature, weaving in and out of pleasure and food gardens, folklore, songs and myths.

Vines also are a much larger and more diverse group of plants than you might think if you judged from the offerings of most nurseries and garden centers. Even the best local firms rarely sell more climbing species than you can count on the fingers of two hands. The selection by mail is better, but still unworthy of a category of plants that is both ornamental and practical. Seed and plant companies are unlikely to sell in excess of two dozen ornamental climbers, yet they may list 50 marigold varieties and an equal number of tea roses. Still, the selection by mail is the best available to gardeners. By shopping from more than one catalog, including those from firms like Forestfarm, Steffen's, J. L. Hudson and the British seed house Chiltern, it is possible to purchase both plants and seeds of many climbing species.

There are vines for all tastes and requirements: vines prized for their flower, their fruit or their leaf; vines valued for their screening ability or their open growth; vines that are perennial or annual, deciduous or evergreen; vines that grow rapidly or slowly, that flourish in sun or shade, in dry or wet; vines that stoutly adhere to surfaces or those that want help as they clamber upward. Vines, handsome and useful, should be among the first of the gardener's plant choices.

The natural grace of most climbers is endemic—poetry isn't full of lovers trysting in ivy-covered bowers without reason. There is a slew of nonwandering plants (flowering dogwood and copper beech come immediately to mind) that are beautifully structured, inherently elegant. But for every simple, graceful *Narcissus poeticus* there is a Dutch hyacinth, stiff and relentlessly formal. Among vines, fortunately, there are few hyacinths. Moreover, there are spectacular flowers—brilliantly septaled clematis, pendulous racemes of wisteria, showy morning glory trumpets, exotically shaped passionflowers. There is fragrance, too, ornamental berries and handsome seedpods.

Despite their varied beauty, vines are usually recommended only for their usefulness. "The description may be accurate," garden historian Tyler Whittle laments, "but it is belittling." Vines deserve to be planted for their intrinsic qualities; their ability to camouflage is of secondary importance. "What matters," he writes, "is the plant."

Whittle is correct; nonetheless, the usefulness of vines should not be discounted. "A physician," Frank Lloyd Wright observed, "may bury his mistakes, but an architect can only plant a vine." Like charity, vines cover a multitude of sins—the uninspired designs of buildings, rusting gutters and downspouts, ugly antenna cables and wires, the chipped woodwork of a sunny window. These and other eyesores can be artfully obscured by an upsweep of leaf and bloom. Mirabel Osler praises the masking qualities of vines in *A Gentle Plea for Chaos* (1989), her love song to the spontaneous and natural. "What a pity more house walls aren't covered," she writes, ". . . for how well plants diffuse the red of bricks, the disagreeable texture of stucco or the bleakness of concrete." As for gardeners lucky enough not to inhabit a box masquerading as a home or a neo-Victorian conglomeration, one of those mix-and-match houses spawned by computer architects, they can feel smug and use vines to adorn rather than to veil.

Experienced gardeners know that vines have an immutable way of anchoring the vertical to the horizontal, linking

The heart-shaped foliage of annual morning glories, Ipomoea *spp., neatly overlaps to create an attractive, intransparent screen that gives privacy to a yard or garden.*

built structures to the land. Neither flowers nor trees so complete a house as does a luxuriant vine, tying the home down and suggesting permanence and grace. Using vines around doorways and windows is an old, familiar trick, although the effect is not always successful. "Frequently we see a cottage with a door in the centre, and one window on each side, and vines trained over the sashes," Susan Fenimore Cooper, daughter of the American novelist, writes in *Rural Hours* (1850), "which gives it an odd look, like a house in green spectacles . . . ." A thoughtful gardener, though, can deck a house with climbers without transforming it into an ocular topiary.

With the aid of supports, climbing plants can enclose and frame the garden in an arresting way. The communal yard is an invention of twentieth-century suburban democracy. Colonial Americans invariably fenced their gardens, often adorning those fences with Virginia creeper and honeysuckle or with practical choices like grapes or gourds. Although most of us have no cattle to close out, we can secure a degree of privacy and create the same pretty effect on our walls and fences, cloaking even galvanized metal with the lush beauty of a sturdy vine.

Vines also help the ardent compensate for a small garden, for they permit additional foliage and blossom, expand the apparent size, yet require almost no space. What is surprising, in this era of decks, balconies, patios, roof gardens and Lilliputian lots, is that gardeners have directed so little of their attention to varieties that rise. Similarly, professional plant breeders, preoccupied with dwarfing large species and turning graceful, wandering plants into turgid clumps, have overlooked the fact that ramblers are ideal for small gardens. Some species, such as Japanese honeysuckle (*Lonicera*

The sweet, tubular blossoms of honeysuckle, Lonicera *spp., are irresistible to bees.*

japonica), are too vigorous for a pocket-sized yard, but many of its less aggressive cousins are ideal for those who are rich in garden dreams but are land poor.

Development of Vines

It was the limits of nature—of space, climate, moisture, soil, competition and light—that likely gave rise to vines in the first place. Rather than a distinct botanical group, like dicotyledons or monocotyledons, vines are a behavioral group, plants that adapted to their environment by becoming scandent. As cacti were forced by desert conditions to discard their leaves and move the process of photosynthesis to their stems, vines elongated their stems in a race to the sun. (Since they depended on other plants and structures for support, their stems also became less fibrous and increasingly hollow—long, limber pipes designed to carry water and food from the roots to the leaves.) It is possible that the

ascending impulses of vines were also adaptive reactions to other threats: just as some plants developed thorns or bitter sap to avoid being consumed by animals, vines may have increased the distance between nodes, the points on the stem where leaves form, in order to move their fruit out of reach of predators. And to make their flowers more accessible for pollination by insects and birds.

Whatever the specific causes, the overtly adaptive behavior of vining plants was seized by Charles Darwin as yet another example of natural competition and the battle for survival. Darwin was led to the subject of vines by the American botanist Asa Gray, who had written about the tendril movements of cucurbitaceous plants in 1858. In 1865, Darwin published "The Movements and Habits of Climbing Plants" in the *Journal of the Linnean Society*; nearly two decades later, he expanded his original essay into a 200-page book, again arguing that plants evolved into climbers because of competition. "Plants become climbers, in order, as it may be presumed, to reach the light, and to expose a large surface of their leaves to its action and to that of the free air."

Forgoing sleep to observe a ceropegia, Darwin recorded its efforts to find support—movement so purposeful, so like the movement of animals, that it seemed as if the vine were able to think. "It was an interesting spectacle to watch the long shoot sweeping this grand circle, night and day, in search of some object round which to twine," he wrote. Plants, he concluded, display the power of movement when it is to their advantage; their movement showed "how high in the scale of organization a plant may rise."

The elliptical motion of twining plants, called circumnutation, can be clockwise or counterclockwise, depending on the species. The path is typically at a right angle to the source of light or heat. Twining plants, if turned upside down, will uncoil and recircle their supports, and a vine that is pulled away from a support will reseek the object. If the gardener guides a vine in the "wrong" direction, the plant will rewind itself. Japanese wisteria (*Wisteria floribunda*), for instance, twines from right to left; Chinese wisteria (*W. sinensis*), left to right. If trained incorrectly, I discovered the hard way, wisteria will undo the gardener's work, slowing its development in the process.

How Vines Climb

Not all vines are twiners, however. There are at least two dozen distinct ways that vines climb, although most are variants of five basic methods: vines that scramble, that catch with thorns, that weave or twine, that root and that clasp. The differences are somewhat artificial and not terribly important, except in that understanding the methods enables the gardener to provide an appropriate support. No clematis, for instance, is going to climb a bare wall, as English ivy (*Hedera helix*) will. Porcelain berry, with its glorious crackled-blue fruit and unpronounceable scientific name (*Ampelopsis brevipedunculata*) is best grown against a netted trellis, either wire or cord, and even then it may need to be coaxed in the beginning to attach its tendrils.

But in a propitious setting—their heads in the sun, their feet in the shade, the country wisdom goes—most vines grow quickly and ask for little assistance. As a friend cautioned when giving me a small wisteria cutting, "Plant it and stand back!" The English herbalist John Gerard sounded a similar alarm 400 years ago, warning that the cucumber "creepes alongst upon the ground all about." And so it was when I grew an heirloom cucumber, one Gerard might have known, variously called 'Apple Shape,' 'True Lemon' and 'Lemon Apple' because of its round, yellow fruit. Like a malevolent snake, my cucumber vine crept over the beans and tomatoes, over the squash and onions, crept through the grass and climbed the raspberries, and seemed game to keep creeping until I finally brought it to bay with the sharp blades of a Lawn-Boy.

Other than climbing roses, which come with backpointing thorns that will catch on any convenient surface, most commonly grown vines are either species that adhere to vertical surfaces ("cleaveth wonderful hard," one sixteenth-century writer put it) or plants that twine, with either stem, leaf or tendril. Adhering or rooting vines, such as climbing hydrangea (*Hydrangea anomala petiolaris*) and Boston ivy (*Parthenocissus tricuspidata*), need little more than a vertical surface to ascend; twiners require a broken support, and some species benefit from being tied or secured.

There is also a whole other group of climbing plants or, more accurately, plants that have been coerced into flattening themselves against walls and trellises: espaliers. The word, from the Italian *spalle*, for shoulder, once referred sole-

Equipped with adhering aerial roots, climbing hydrangea ascends walls without help.

The colorful bloom and contrasting foliage of a climbing plant, like large-flowered clematis hybrids, can effectively break the monotony of a fence or the wall of a building.

ly to the technique; today the term espalier is used to describe either the technique or the plant.

Pears and apples are the traditional plants that are pruned and trained into the set patterns—palmette verriers, vertical cordons, Belgian fences and more—but espalier isn't limited to fruit trees. Pyracantha, forsythia and magnolias are among the many ornamentals that are strong-armed into botanical bondage. Vines like ivy and wisteria are popular subjects too, disciplined into garlands and grids. Artificial yet stunning, espalier transforms shrubs and trees into vines, a testament to the merits of climbers if ever there were one. (Pleaching, or intertwining, trees and shrubs to create a dense screen or to cover walkways, is another witness for the useful and handsome effect that vines produce naturally.)

Highly ornamental and stylized, espal-

ier also has a practical side: by planting against protective walls, gardeners are able to expand the range of plants they grow, able to cultivate species that otherwise would be too tender to survive. It is a reminder that when choosing vines to plant against a sunny wall or another solid support, it is possible to succeed with species that officially are classed as appropriate only for warmer gardens. Thanks to a brick wall and a southern exposure, a Minnesota gardener I know harvests 'Red Haven' peaches almost every summer.

Vine Supports

Providing a good home for vines can be an opportunity to introduce an interesting built element into the garden—a lamppost, a wooden fence, a stone wall, an intricate trellis, a romantic archway. Or, on a more ambitious scale, a pergola or arbor. Some gardeners use living supports like trees and shrubs to support climbers. Vita Sackville-West, the English garden writer, was famous for draping plants with plants, a kind of horticultural layering that readers of *Vogue* would recognize. She recommended old hedges—"too heavy a job to grub out, too expensive to replace"—as ideal props for vines: "I can imagine *Clematis montana*, either the white or pink, throwing itself like a cloak over the top of the hedge; a single plant of this should cover an area of 15 feet within a very few years." Or trees: "What we tend to forget is that nature provides some far higher reaches into which we can shoot long festoons whose beauty gains from the transparency of dangling in mid-air."

Supports can be simple or complex, purchased or homemade, but they need to be strong. For several years, I've been growing clematis up fencing salvaged from an old dog pen. Called pig wire in England, it works well, and its rusted brown color blends nicely with the wood shingles of my house. Other gardeners use string, plastic pea netting, chicken wire, poles, wood and pipe. I run morning glories (*Ipomoea* spp.) and hyacinth beans (*Dolichos lablab*) up heavy strings, because I grow them as annuals; in contrast, most perennial climbers want supports that will last for many seasons. Garden stores now offer, in addition to traditionally designed lath trellises, interesting new supports for climbing plants fashioned from modern, durable materials. There is an assortment of prefabricated hoops, fans and archways, as well as books and magazines, that overflow with plans for trellises, pergolas and arbors. For the record, an arbor, which evolved hand in hand with the cultivation of the grapevine, is nothing more than an overhead trellis, a shaded retreat. A pergola, which also provides shade, traditionally is a walkway that consists of columns and overhead horizontal beams, a construction known as a lang in the Orient.

As for growing vines directly on buildings, the usual advice is, don't. Climbers, especially those that attach with rootlets, scar wood and may damage the mortar. On the other hand, if you have a wall that won't hold paint, as I once did, an independent climber like ivy is the answer to your prayers. And if your mortar is in good condition—you can't crumble it with your fingernail—it's unlikely that any vine is going to destroy it during your lifetime. This may be one of those occasions when it's acceptable to be selfish: enjoy the ivy and leave the mortar and paint problems to the house's next owners.

Vine Versatility

Gardeners, especially those living in temperate zones, may witness arborescence, a mature vine's taking on the characteristics of a tree. More often, however, vines remain frustrated trees, incorporating many of the tree's merits but thwarted by their weak stems from becoming towering oaks, able to stand independently. Still, they grow up, sometimes 30 feet or more, and with the help of a support, they provide shade. Nothing could be more picturesque than lunching on a stone terrace canopied by grapevines, the sun delicately filtering through the leaves, just catching the maroon of the fruit. If you plan on vegetation to roof a living area, however, you may wish to forgo parts of this romantic scene and avoid vines with heavy, long-lasting bloom or with sweet fruit—thereby forgoing the bees that they will attract.

Or climbers, if you prefer, can scale but not roam, keeping the garden sunny yet providing flower and leaf where they normally are lacking. Many vines, like trees, live for decades, but with the advantage of reaching maturity rapidly. Most take only one, two or three years to bloom and fruit, rather than ten or twenty. We can plant vines for our children *and* ourselves.

Some vines are also willing to serve as ground covers, rambling and crawling over eroding banks and played-out dirt, masking areas where grass is not practical, possible or desirable. But English ivy, which is often thought of exclusively as a ground cover, and other vines will follow their upgoing instincts when they encounter a vertical guide, and many climbing plants are not as tidy or uniform as are traditional covers like pachysandra and vinca. Still, Virginia creeper (*Parthenocissus quinquefolia*), Hall's honeysuckle (*Lonicera japonica* 'Halliana'), five-leaf akebia (*Akebia quinata*), winter creeper (*Euonymus* spp.) and bittersweet (*Celastrus scandens*), as well as most ivies, are among the vines that capably double as ground covers.

Many climbers—honeysuckle, trumpet

Some vines, like this English ivy, Hedera helix, *can take over unless pruned regularly.*

creeper (*Campsis* spp.) clematis and bittersweet, to name only a few—have flowers and fruit that are attractive to wildlife, especially birds. Birds also seek out vines for shelter, finding harbor in the dense growth of climbing plants. House finches nest annually in the Boston ivy over an Ohio friend's back door, unintimidated by her perpetual coming and going. With a small frame and a fast-growing vine—hops (*Humulus lupulus*) or scarlet runner beans (*Phaseolus coccineus*) work nicely—you can create a cozy summer habitat for a dreamy child, a perfect haven when bedtime comes too soon.

A few vines, well behaved in Duluth, just won't play in Peoria; or, more accurately, play too loudly in Peoria. Like the weed in the overworked definition—a flower growing in the wrong place—some climbing species are too rampant for certain microclimates. American bittersweet is manageable in the far North, one of the few vines that will grow in USDA Zone 2, but it destroys nearly everything it encounters on Cape Cod. Wild morning glory (*Calystegia sepium*), once established in a congenial environment, is almost impossible to dislodge. It isn't called man-under-ground, bindweed and devil's vine for nothing. Cutting off its top only encourages its roots, and chopping its roots only makes more plants.

Even wisteria, widely planted in many regions, can creep under shingles, pry loose gutters and obscure windows. A friend of mine has a wisteria that has magically pierced the insulated wall of her house and is now cheerfully growing inside a second-floor bedroom. She is allowing it to roam simply to satisfy her curiosity as to what it will do next. In *For a Herbarium* (1948), the French novelist Colette labeled wisteria a despot, incoercible and rampageous. The wisteria of her childhood home, she relates, came into contact with a honeysuckle, itself not a timid species, and ''slowly strangled it as a snake suffocates a bird."

Vines to Avoid

Eclipsing the subtleties of microclimates are at least two vines that gardeners should shun: poison ivy (*Rhus toxicodendron*) and kudzu (*Pueraria lobata*). The agonies of the first are widely known, and it is wise to be equally familiar with its leaf—"leaflets three, let it be"—in order to avoid an accidental encounter and weeks of misery. This vine can climb, ramble as a ground cover or grow erect in bush form. It is the oil in the plant's roots, stems, leaves and berries that is toxic; even dead plants are unsafe to touch.

Imported from Japan for use in soil conservation, kudzu has exploded through the North American countryside. Smothering everything in its path, it has proved more devastating to the native flora of the southern United States than was General Sherman. Fortunately, kudzu, "the plant that ate Dixie," grows only as an annual in most northern zones.

Also to be avoided are most parasitic vines, plants that take their living from other plants. A close relative of the morning glory, the leafless dodder (*Cuscuta gronovii*) strangles its host. Ironically known as love vine—or not ironically, depending on your experience—this climber attaches itself to another plant and then invades it, sucking the nourishment it needs. Once the connection is made, the roots of this botanical Dracula wither away, no longer necessary for the plant's survival. Although the dodder is covered with white flowers, no informed gardener would plant it. But another native semiparasite, mistletoe (*Phoradendron serotinum*) is more problematic. Although its leaves contain chlorophyll and produce food, mistletoe does tap through its host tree's bark with a modified root, or haustorium, in order to obtain water and minerals. The haustorium does no seri-

Kudzu has smothered the native flora in some regions of the southern United States.

ous harm, but being shaded by the mistletoe's foliage may affect the host. The wonderful berries are hard to resist, but plant mistletoe away from trees and shrubs that you value.

Vine Culture

Happily for gardeners, many admirable climbers are as resourceful and hearty as are these undesirables. What a delight it is to grow plants that likely need to be slowed rather than pampered, snipped rather than coaxed. Even vines, however, cannot flourish without the basic requirements of good soil and adequate moisture and light.

A languishing plant may mean the gardener has forgotten that the dirt alongside wall and building foundations, a common home for vines, is frequently backfill, unsuitable for growing much beyond nettles and dandelions. The soil also may be highly alkaline, because of leaching from concrete foundations, and the majority of vines prefer neutral or slightly acid soil. Even clematis, invariably described in garden books as lime-loving plants, do well in neutral or even modestly acid soil.

Remember, too, that nearly all vines are vigorous feeders. After all, these are climbers and creepers, scramblers and ramblers. Compared with most plants, their growth in one season is prodigious. As a result, they demand organically rich, deeply dug soil and benefit from annual doses of compost or well-rotted manure. Some exuberant growers, such as silver lace vine (*Polygonum aubertii*), should be fed twice a year. Most experts recommend a fertilizer that is low in nitrogen, unless lush foliage is the goal. Bonemeal, which is high in phosphorus and low in nitrogen, is a good additive for many vines. In northern climates, climbing species also may profit from being mulched in winter with compost or peat mixed with soil.

If the vine's support is both solid and tall—or if it is set beneath an overhang, which it shouldn't be—it is possible that little rainfall or sun will reach the plant. No climber, not even the most lusty, will flourish without enough light and water. Solid supports like stone walls also can block the circulation of air, leaving plants susceptible to diseases like powdery mildew. Finally, as a general rule, the harsher the climate, the less vigorous a vine's growth and bloom. Gardeners in the far North may convince a wisteria to survive, but it is unlikely to excel: leaves will be small and flowers few.

The good news is that most climbers are resistant to disease and insects. Climbing roses, at least the majority of modern cultivars, are heir to all the plagues that visit twentieth-century roses; Virginia creeper attracts the Japanese beetle, a bug no one wants to invite into the garden. But most other ornamental vines are remarkably problem free. Climbers and ramblers in the vegetable garden are somewhat more susceptible, as are vines grown indoors where scale, mealy bugs and whiteflies flourish. But as a group, climbing plants are astonishingly unaffected by the bugs and illnesses that devastate their garden and windowsill neighbors.

Pruning and Propagation

Not every vine hurls itself up as fast as Jack's bean did. For example, climbing hydrangea, as an old White Flower Farm catalog diplomatically put it, is "a bit slow to establish itself." White Flower Farm was accurate: my 6-inch plants didn't budge for three years. But most vines are forthright and vigorous, which makes pruning necessary, especially if the garden or the support is small. Pruning also encourages branching and flowering, and it is the sensible recourse for a hopelessly overgrown vine or one full of dead wood. Annual climbers are rarely cut back, but nearly all perennial vines are likely to need regular pruning.

It's a good idea to check a garden encyclopedia before you begin slicing away—some species have unusual requirements—but there are a few general guidelines worth remembering. Always use clean, sharp tools and always cut just above a leaf or stem node. The best time to prune normally depends on when the vine flowers. Plants that bloom on the current season's shoots, like silver lace vine, are pruned in late winter or early spring. Species that blossom on last season's growth, including spring-blooming clematis species like *C. montana*, are pruned as soon as they finish flowering. Perennial vines that are grown for their foliage, such as Dutchman's pipe (*Aristolochia durior*), can be pruned at the gardener's convenience. Some foliage vines, like Boston ivy, may lose their leaves in winter and appear dead. Come spring, however, they

'Dorothy Perkins,' a slow-growing rambler rose, requires some assistance to climb.

flowers, is applicable to few perennial vines. Grafting and budding are sometimes used to propagate vines, usually hybrids or species that germinate poorly or are difficult to root from cuttings.

Most perennial climbers are propagated rather easily by rooting softwood cuttings in sand. After rooting, the cuttings are potted and overwintered in a cold frame, then transplanted in spring to a permanent location in the garden. An even easier rooting method, called layering, is to allow a vine to root itself by making cuts along a stem and pegging it in soil. Once rooting occurs, you can sever that stem section from the parent plant and transplant it. Vines, because of their elongated stems, are ideal candidates for serpentine layering, pegging the stem in more than one place in order to produce many new plants.

Having complained before that too few climbing plants are easily available for purchase, I must admit that some of the most common vines are also the most choice. They should not be excluded simply because they are familiar. In my Vermont garden, I grow the everyday— Boston ivy, clematis 'Nelly Moser,' 'Heavenly Blue' morning glory—alongside the uncustomary, plants like porcelain berry, wild cucumber vine (*Echinocystis lobata*) and the Russian Virgin's bower (*Clematis tangutica*). In the following chapters, four garden masters lobby for their favorites. Their choices may not be yours. But as to including climbing plants in our gardens, a second-rank poet once wrote that "on heaven's wall a golden vine clambers bright." If he is correct, the afterlife is filled with smart gardeners. We should take a page from their book.

bounce back to life, so don't be premature with the clippers.

Getting a vine to go where you want it isn't a difficult job, but it is a task that must begin in the spring. Once the 'Comtesse de Bouchard' has woven herself into a tangled mass, the chances of guiding her neatly upward are small. Like delphiniums, which must be staked from the start rather than trussed up after they have flopped over, vines should be guided from the beginning. As soon as they have direction, most require little more help.

Annual and edible vines are typically started from seed, either sown directly in the garden or sown indoors and transplanted once the danger of frost is past. Some perennial vines like climbing hydrangea can be grown from seed, but only species will come true, and germination often requires both stratifying the seed and meeting specific temperature, light, moisture and soil requirements. Division, so successful with perennial

Karan Davis Cutler is Senior Editor of *Harrowsmith Country Life* magazine and writes a weekly garden column for two Vermont newspapers.

Morning glory, Ipomoea *spp.*

Chapter Two:
Annual Vines

By Jennifer Bennett

magine Tarzan swinging through the jungle and you have grasped the essence of tropical vines: rampant, prolific, as thick as your wrist and strong enough to hold Johnny Weismuller. Some tropical vines are slender stemmed, but they too are so wiry that they withstand the power of gravity and wind. These, the flowering vines that Northerners grow as tender annuals, are often perennials in their native lands, capable of reaching the treetops. In a warm greenhouse, too, they may thrive all year, swamping the neighboring geraniums and African violets. ✑ In fact, compared with the number of tropical species, there are few vines that are native to temperate places, especially locations as far north as my garden in Ontario. In part, vines tend to be tropicals because freezing and thawing distorts the circulation of fluids in them, just as it destroys pipes full of water. The plumbing of vines is little short of miraculous. Some species are able to pump water hundreds of feet from the forest floor to the treetops. As any gardener knows, the problem of kinks and knots impeding the flow of water is formidable, even in a 20-foot garden hose.

'Early Spencer' sweet peas, Lathyrus odoratus, *add both color and fragrance to the garden.*

The only well-known flowering annual vine native to the North is the sweet pea (*Lathyrus odoratus*). It grows a few feet tall in a season, a measly achievement compared with the growth rate of some tropicals. The latter climb with almost visible speed in hot summer weather and may be twining about the chimney by season's end, especially if they have the moist, organic soil and the sheltered, lightly shaded situation that suits them best.

They also need support, unless they are going to trail from a hanging basket or window box or hang over the lip of a rock wall. Vines rejoice in upward mobility and grow fastest when they have grasped an appropriate support; exactly what is appropriate varies with the physiology of the vine. If the trellis is more than a few inches from the vine, you should provide the vine with a nearby string, twig or wire that can lead it to its support system. I have grown annual vines on strings, on a wooden lattice, on wire netting encircling the trunk of a fruit tree and from hanging baskets and window boxes. Turid Forsyth, my coauthor for *The Harrowsmith Annual Garden*, which includes a chapter about vines, grew some of the clingers directly on the wall of her house and others on a trellis around her front door. Both of us were impressed by the beauty and speedy growth of these single-season plants, from the well-known morning glory (*Ipomoea* spp.) to the little-known balloon vine (*Cardiospermum halicacabum*) and Chilean glory flower (*Eccremocarpus scaber*).

Annual Vine Culture

Because few annual vine plants are sold by nurseries, you will need to grow them yourself from seed. Keep the tropics in mind when planting and caring for tender climbers. Most require an early start in-

Brightly hued nasturtiums, Tropaeolum majus, *are among the easiest annual vines to grow.*

The clean, open growth of the sunshine-yellow canary creeper, Tropaeolum peregrinum, *is valuable for its ability to enhance but not obscure its support.*

doors, but they are worth the extra trouble in curiosity value alone. I use a purchased seedling mixture, making sure it is thoroughly dampened with room-temperature water before sowing. The soil must never be allowed to dry out before germination occurs. Slipping the seeded containers into a clear plastic bag will conserve moisture, but do not put the bag into direct sun. I favor recycled foam coffee cups as seedling holders, but cell trays and individual pots—peat, plastic or clay—also work well. Any small container with drainage will serve.

After the seeds sprout, move them into bright light—at least 14 hours per day—thin to one strong plant per container, and give the seedlings a weekly feeding of fish fertilizer mixed according to package directions. If the seedlings outgrow their pots before spring frosts have finished, carefully transplant them into individual peat pots or milk cartons full of compost or a half-and-half mixture of topsoil and rotted manure. Many annual vines have fragile root systems that are easily damaged if they are mishandled during transplanting, a reason some growers prefer sowing in peat pots, which can be planted directly in the garden.

Whether you have bought your plants or started your own seedlings, before they can be planted in the garden, they must go through a process of acclimatization called hardening off. The idea is to accustom the plants gradually to outdoor conditions. Plants that have been started indoors, where the air is still, temperatures are fairly constant and light exposures are lower than outdoors, will be set back and may die if planted immediately in a sunny garden.

To avoid this, beginning about two weeks before the scheduled transplantation date, move your flats or pots of seedlings to a sheltered shady spot outside. Keep them there only an hour or so the first day, then for a couple of hours, then

The tender, five-petaled black-eyed Susan vine, Thunbergia alata, *is at its best when its slender stems are allowed to trail gracefully along supports like low walls and fences.*

for the entire day. At the end of the first week, you can begin to place the plants in the sun—only briefly at first, but gradually increasing their exposure until sun-lovers are spending all day in an unshaded location. Once plants are acclimated, setting them in the garden should go without a hitch. The ideal day for transplanting is cool, overcast and humid. If nature doesn't cooperate, be prepared to simulate those conditions by supplying temporary shade and plenty of water.

A few vines—including morning glories, sweet peas, canary creepers and nasturtiums (*Tropaeolum* spp.), and bottle gourds (*Lagenaria* spp.)—develop so rapidly that they will flower in the North even if sown outdoors in early summer. Again, make sure the soil stays moist until the seeds sprout, and thereafter water deeply whenever the top ½ inch of soil is dry. After flowering begins, a feeding of manure tea every two weeks will keep the vine growing strongly.

Given a good start and some warm summer weather, annual vines will bring butterflies, hummingbirds, honeybees and a wind-rustled, perfumed shadiness to short-season gardens. The hoots of monkeys and the shrieks of birds of paradise seem to come from beyond the kitchen door, and the gardener easily imagines a voice within the foliage, stumbling over those famous syllables from distant civilization: "Me, Tarzan."

Asarina spp.

(creeping gloxinia, climbing snapdragon, chickabiddy, hummingbird vine)

There are about 15 species of asarina, all Central American members of the snapdragon family. Asarina means snapdragon in Spanish. Sometimes listed as

Maurandya, all are perennials, but are most easily grown in the North as somewhat hardy annuals. Unlike many other tropical vines, these delight in cool soil and will tolerate fall's colder weather. I once lost a crop of seedlings by placing them in the hot greenhouse sun soon after they had sprouted.

Asarina vines are fragile in appearance, with slender stems that reach about 6 feet in northern gardens. The flowers are small but lovely. *A. antirrhiniflora* bears inch-long red and yellow snapdragonlike blooms. *A. barclaiana* has attractive, soft green foliage and torenialike flowers— white, rose or purple, depending on the cultivar—while *A. scandens* 'Violet Glow' bears longer, indigo-blue flowers. *A. erubescens* has soft, fragrant, downy foliage and rose-pink flowers that are 3 inches or longer.

Sow the seeds early—March is a good time—as the seedlings are tiny and grow slowly at first. Although some packet directions suggest that germination takes two or three weeks, I found that the seeds of *A. scandens* sprouted in less than a week after being sown on the soil surface of containers that I then slipped into a clear plastic bag and kept at room temperature. Sown in the same manner, the pepperlike seeds of *A. antirrhiniflora* sprouted in 18 days, as did those of *A. barclaiana*, whose eccremocarpuslike seeds I covered lightly.

When all danger of frost is past, set the plants into containers or in the ground, a foot apart, at the base of a lattice or arbor. The vines begin flowering about 18 weeks after sowing and will continue to blossom until heavy fall frost, provided dead flowers and seedpods are removed.

Cardiospermum halicacabum

(balloon vine, love-in-a-puff)

This delightful, tropical American annual vine sports tiny white, five-petaled flowers that magically transform themselves into seedpods that are mammoth in comparison: three-sided, papery balls a good inch wide, two or three per peduncle, or stalk. The balls are so lightweight that they bob up and down in the wind. Every ball holds three seeds, each of which is black at maturity and marked with a heart-shaped white spot that gives the genus its name. At this stage, the seeds can be saved for next year.

About three weeks before the last frost, file the hard seeds lightly, soak them overnight and then sow them ½-inch deep in individual containers kept at room temperature. Germination should occur in about a week. After the last frost, set the plants a foot apart in rich soil.

Balloon vines have tendrils that will twine around a trellis or strings, providing a light screen of slender stems and soft, semiglossy, tomatolike foliage. The short tendrils are modified flower peduncles,

In his book about vines, Charles Darwin called *C. scandens* "an excellently constructed climber" because its tendrils, almost a foot long, travel in wide sweeps as they search for something to hold. They culminate in sharp hooks that "readily catch soft wood or gloves or the skin of the naked hand." Thus the vine, which can reach 20 feet in a summer, will hang onto almost anything—strings, wires, a trellis or even crevices in a wall— and the oval, purple-veined leaves create the effect of a massive plant.

Start this vine early, as it does not grow rapidly until the weather is warm and requires about four months to move from seed to flower. Germination may take longer than 14 days, so it should be started in early March. I plant two or three seeds per pot, thinning to one. After the last

never more than an inch long, that curl downward into hooks. These plants are not speedy climbers. Charles Darwin noted that the tendrils took as long as 24 hours to curl twice around a thin twig— some ipomoeas, by contrast, made a circle in less than three hours. My vine grew to 8 feet by the end of July, then another 2 feet by summer's end.

Cobaea scandens

(cup-and-saucer vine, cathedral bells)

Another horticultural conversation piece, this rampant Central American tender perennial produces five-cornered, papery green buds that open into "saucers" holding elegant fluted "cups" some 2½ inches deep. The entire tea set hangs upside down.

The flowers are a study for time-lapse photographers: they open pale green, gradually turn lilac and then become purple with longitudinal white stripes. Although large, the blooms are not showy because their color blends with that of the foliage and stems. There is also a white-flowering cultivar, 'Alba.'

spring frost, I transplant the seedlings outdoors, 2 feet apart in rich soil. Cool June weather so discouraged a vine I grew last year on a trellised archway that it did not flower until the end of August, not long before it was stopped by the first frost. If this vine grows on a wall with some protection, however, it will continue blooming for many weeks.

Eccremocarpus scaber

(Chilean glory flower)

Schools of modest flowers that resemble inch-long, open-mouthed goldfish, not only orange but also pink, red, yellow and bicolored, decorate the stem tips of this lovely South American tender perennial. Their color, unique shape and ability to last in the vase make the Chilean glory flower a frequent choice among flower arrangers and gardeners. The slender vine has a twining stem, tendrils and petioles and also tiny hooks that enable it to hang onto trellis or wall. The slightly hairy,

roundish leaves are soft green and deeply notched.

Eccremocarpus has black seeds encased in flat papery coatings, looking a little like fried eggs. I lightly cover them and keep the pots warm and out of bright light. Packet directions indicate a one- or two-month sprouting time at room temperature, but my seeds generally sprout in about a week. Start these in early March, as the seedlings are tiny and need about four months to flower.

Plants set outdoors in well-manured soil after the last frost should be about 6 feet tall by early August, and may reach 10 feet before heavy frost. One flowered in my garden until early November, when a temperature of 5 degrees F finally killed it.

Ipomoea alba

(moonflower)

This evening-flowering version of the morning glory resembles its cousin in many ways. It is a large-leafed, heavy, twining plant that grows rampantly from big seeds. Moonflowers are lovely for patio pots, whether you grow just one plant in a foot-wide pot of compost, or several on a trellis by a bedroom window. There the moonlike flowers—big, round and white—that open just after sunset can be enjoyed best. Their sweet fragrance attracts night-flying moths, whose long, unfurling tongues amazingly reach the nectar at the base of the 4-inch trumpets.

By afternoon the day after they open, the flowers will have wilted, but buds will continue to form until frost, which kills the plant swiftly. The Thompson & Morgan seed catalog suggests that stems holding buds can be cut for evening flower arrangements, an enticing idea. The large leaves, as wide as 8 inches, form a dense screen when the vine is guided up strings set a foot apart.

Gardening books sometimes advise that moonflower seeds be scraped or

the genus, is the morning glory, classed only as *Ipomoea*, though there are several species distinguishable chiefly by flower color. There are also dwarf cultivars suitable for hanging baskets. The morning glory is the most popular annual vine in North America because it is showy, dependable and easily grown from seeds sown directly in the garden from early May to June.

Morning glories will take with equal delight to strings, fence wire or lattice, and will also drape becomingly over stumps and compost bins. I soak the big seeds in tepid water overnight before sowing them about ½ inch deep near the trellis or support where they will grow. Or sow them indoors a month earlier, one seed per cell or pot, then transplant them outdoors after the last frost, spaced about a foot apart. They are drought tolerant and will grow in poor soil, but grow more lushly if the dirt is rich.

The flowers, which may be as wide as 5 inches, open in the morning and last

nicked before planting. I have sown the seeds scraped and unscraped and had identical germination rates. It does help, however, to soak the apple-piplike seeds overnight before sowing them, about ½ inch deep, in a warm spot indoors about six to eight weeks before the last frost. They should sprout in less than a week. Carefully transplant them outdoors after all danger of frost has passed. (The seeds can also be sown directly outdoors, in the manner of morning glories.) Mine, planted outdoors the second week in May, were in bloom by early August.

Ipomoea spp.

(morning glory)

The genus *Ipomoea* is large, with perhaps 500 species, and has spawned a confusion of offshoots that may be called not only *Ipomoea* but also *Quamoclit, Calonyction* and *Mina*. All of these genera are frost-sensitive, twining, tender perennials that appreciate a sheltered, sunny place with warm, humus-rich soil.

The best known of the bunch, displaying the typical funnel-shaped flowers of

only a day—a schedule typical of the genus—though buds will continue to form until cold temperatures arrive. Morning glories appreciate a feeding of fish fertilizer every two weeks throughout summer and travel 8 to 10 feet by the time of the first frost, which rapidly kills them.

Lagenaria spp.

(bottle gourd)

Bottle gourds are fun to grow and are a good project for children, as their seeds can be sown directly in the garden. As soon as hot weather comes, the vines tumble over fences, stumps and trellises with glorious abandon, coloring their small world with soft green leaves, scented white flowers and fruits that turn from green, when they are edible, to beige, when their hard shells can be carved or painted according to one's fancy.

I do not always harvest a crop of mature bottles, but when I do, a crop of birdhouses and feeders is the happy result. Bottle gourds have been used for centuries as urns, bowls, spoons, flasks and musical instruments. They are highly durable, much more so than the yellow or orange gourds produced on vines of the genus *Cucurbita*. I have had birdhouse rejects, nearly as tough as polystyrene cups, last a couple of years in the compost pile.

To increase my odds of harvesting mature gourds, I sow the seeds indoors about a month before the last spring frost, ½ inch deep in individual pots. Once the nights are warm, I transplant them outside to a sunny, sheltered place, a foot or so apart in good soil. Bottle gourds have twining stems and long tendrils that allow them to hang onto strings, wires or branches. During the warmest summer weather the plants may grow 6 inches a day, and they can reach more than 30 feet by fall frost. Let the bottles mature on the vine or pick them when almost mature and allow them to dry indoors. Before

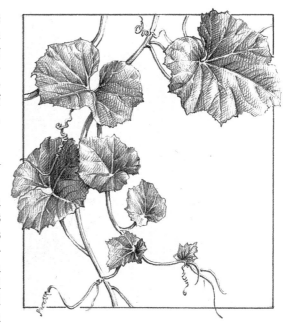

carving, wash them in a solution of household bleach and water to kill any mold on the skin.

Lathyrus odoratus

(sweet pea)

The heady sweetness of this flower and its complexity of shape have made it a favorite of gardeners in England, where seed companies offer scores of varieties and gardeners vie for the tallest, earliest, most prolific vines. The climate of that country suggests the conditions sweet peas favor—damp and cool. Unlike the other annual garden vines, sweet peas are natives of the temperate Mediterranean region, so they will tolerate frost. In fact, like edible peas, they actually relish the cool weather of early spring.

The garden-wise English have come up with many ways to grow the best sweet peas, including digging trenches 2 feet deep, sowing the seeds in the bottom and gradually filling the trenches with well-rotted manure as the vines grow. Nothing so tiring is necessary if you are not entering a contest, but sweet peas do fare best

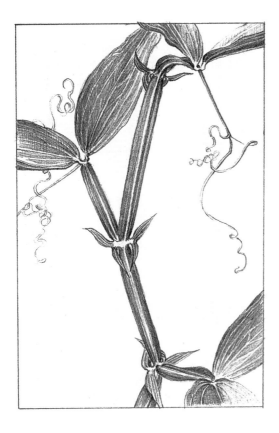

Ipomoea quamoclit

(cypress vine)

Among the lesser-known members of the family *Convolvulaceae*, which includes morning glories and moonflowers, are several small-flowered, slender, twining vines native to tropical America. The cypress vine (*I. quamoclit/Quamoclit pennata*) has needlelike leaves, as suggested by the common name cypress vine. Each funneled flower is just over an inch long, widening into a scarlet, five-pointed star. The anthers within are tipped with contrasting white pollen. (A cousin, the crimson star glory [*Mina lobata*] produces garlands of inch-long flowers that open red and gradually fade through pleasant transformations of orange through yellow to white. Mine bloomed late, and was lovely. The species name describes the handsome lobed leaves, which may be as wide as 3 inches.)

The brown seeds of cypress vine can be sown directly outdoors in warm soil at the

in good, organic soil. In choosing a cultivar, be wary of those that lack fragrance and of some dwarf varieties that have no tendrils and thus cannot climb.

Soak the big seeds overnight before sowing them an inch deep and 4 inches apart; germination takes about a week. Sweet peas hold on by tendril and so require slender supports. Chicken wire works well, as do twigs or strings—the same supports one might use for garden peas. Most varieties, aside from the dwarfs, will grow about 6 feet high. It's a good idea to mulch the roots with straw or grass clippings to keep the soil cool.

The flowers, which appear about six weeks after sowing, are excellent for cutting, and much breeding energy has gone into the creation of longer stems for easier arranging. Continual cutting will keep the plants blooming until the hottest weather. 'Old Spice Mixture' is an especially heat-resistant variety.

end of May or early June, or they can be started indoors four weeks earlier and set outdoors once nights are warm. I soak the hard seeds overnight before sowing them; after sowing, I cover them lightly and keep them at room temperature or warmer. They should sprout in about a week. Scraping the seed, though recommended by some sources, made no difference in germination speed or rate.

Cypress vine is extremely cold sensitive. *M. lobata* seedlings I set into an outdoor pot in mid-May were killed by a nighttime drop to a couple of degrees above freezing, a temperature that did no damage to a moonflower or several other tropicals. Additional seeds sown in pots indoors and in a container outdoors sprouted in six days to two weeks. Set these vines 6 to 8 inches apart in rich soil in a sunny or partly shady, sheltered place and don't let them dry out when still young.

Cypress vines grow as tall as 25 feet, but do not create a mass effect on a trellis; rather, they are airy and cling closely to their support, which makes them wonderfully suitable for twining on a porch or balcony or for climbing the wires of a hanging basket. The slightest frost, be warned, will kill them.

Rhodochiton atrosanguineum

(purple bell vine)

The flowers of this Mexican vine undergo an interesting metamorphosis: from each little bell, which is a long-lasting calyx, a purple horse's nose gradually descends. This is the true flower, and it, in turn, opens to become a smaller bell, so that the whole arrangement resembles a fuchsia a little more than an inch long. Each double bell flower hangs on its own thread from the main stem, a silent chime waving with the slightest breeze.

The flat, papery seeds, which look like those of eccremocarpus, should be planted indoors—lightly covered—about

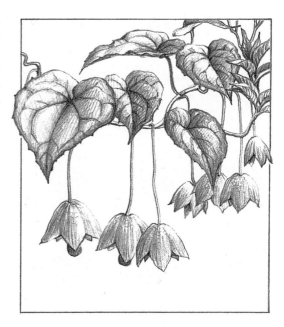

two months before the last frost date. If the soil is kept moist and the pots set in a warm place under clear plastic, the seeds should sprout in about two weeks. After the danger of frost has passed, set the plants into containers or 1 foot apart in good soil in a sheltered, partly shaded location. Blooming usually begins about two months after the plants are moved outdoors.

Purple bell vine is one of the less vigorous tropical climbers. The central stem likes to twine around a slender support such as twine, as do the petioles, but the vine reaches only about 5 feet by early August and may be much smaller if the roots are restricted. Both traits make it an excellent choice for growing in a hanging basket.

Beth Chatto, who owns a famous English nursery called Unusual Plants, calls this "the most exciting" of the tender climbers she has recently discovered. "It would be the loveliest idea to train this plant up and around a pillar in a conservatory, since once started, it flowers under cover long into the winter months."

Thunbergia alata

(black-eyed Susan vine)

Daisies on a vine—at least they look like that from a distance. Almost too neatly fashioned to be true and on stems only a few feet long, this African native is a favorite for hanging baskets and window boxes, though it will twine around strings or wires or just as happily tumble over a stump or fence. In fact, thunbergia is not a true daisy, but a member of the acanthus family. Its center is not composed of a disk of florets, as is the case with a daisy, but is the entrance to a fragile trumpet.

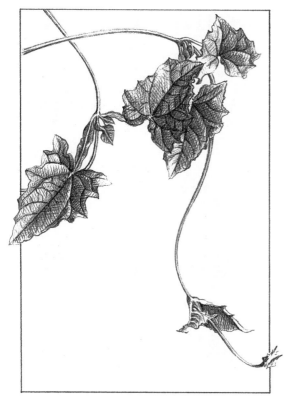

Two months before the last frost, I sow the big, brown seeds about ¼ inch deep, two or three to a pot, thinning to one per pot after they sprout in about two weeks. Then I set the plants into containers approximately 6 inches apart in a sheltered, partly shaded place. Seeds also can be sown directly outdoors around the time of the last spring frost. Young plants that are moved outdoors when the weather has settled will produce buds within a couple of weeks after nights become warm. The stems are winged, and leaves are softly hairy and pointed. On strings or wires, black-eyed Susan forms a dense screen of foliage and flowers.

Unlike most daisies, thunbergia does not do well in the hottest summer weather. Because the vine is a tender perennial, it is capable of surviving indoors by a bright window over the winter, to be moved out again in spring, provided it is gradually hardened off before each journey.

The most commonly grown variety is orange with a deep purple-black center, but there are white and yellow varieties as well, some lacking the characteristic dark center. 'Angel Wings,' unlike most cultivars, has lightly fragrant blooms.

Tropaeolum majus

(climbing nasturtium)

What the mounding nasturtium offers as a ground cover, the climbing version offers to the vertical garden: round, lilypad leaves and five-petaled, tubed flowers in a range of brilliant reds, oranges, yellows, creams and bicolors. These plants, held upright by twining petioles, will create a solid mass of foliage, ideal for sheltering a patio or balcony.

The seeds can be sown a month early indoors in individual pots, but as the plants grow quickly and do not transplant well, the usual routine is to sow seeds outdoors. Like mounding nasturtiums, the climbing types will develop quickly as soon as the temperatures rise, especially if they are given good soil and frequent lukewarm waterings.

I sow two or three seeds ½ inch deep—they need darkness to germinate—and a foot apart at the base of a lattice or of ver-

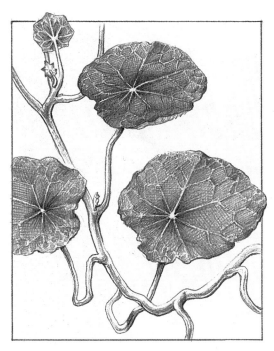

extend from a pale green calyx.

Like a nasturtium, the canary creeper is easy to grow from seed sown directly in warm soil, though the canny gardener can hasten flowering by starting the big, ash-brown seeds indoors a month early. They should sprout in a week or two. Set plants a foot apart, as they will become bushy and create a massive effect, entirely filling in the spaces between strings hung a foot apart. The canary creeper normally grows about 8 or 10 feet tall in a season.

I like this vine in a hanging basket, though it is lush enough to need a foot-wide pot all to itself. Give it rich soil, water plentifully and fertilize once a month. A tender perennial from the Andes, canary

tical strings or wires, then thin to one seedling per station. Seeds sprout in a week or two, and the vine grows 6 to 10 feet in a season. It may become infested by cabbage butterfly larvae, which can be combated with *Bacillus thuringiensis*, or Bt.

The foliage and flowers of vining nasturtiums are edible, with a distinctive peppery flavor, and the seedpods can be pickled like capers. As cut flowers, nasturtiums are long lasting and may even take root in the vase. A South American native, this climber does not mind cool weather, but the first frost will transform it into rags of dead foliage.

Tropaeolum peregrinum

(canary creeper, canarybird vine)

This nasturtium relative is every bit as easy to grow as its better-known cousin and has much prettier foliage: gray-green leaves, 2 or 3 inches wide and deeply lobed, like an open palm. The flowers are a joyful canary yellow and have a shape every bit as interesting as a nasturtium's, with two outstretched, frayed petals that

creeper can be multiplied from cuttings taken in summer or early fall and rooted indoors, where it doubles nicely as a houseplant until spring.

Jennifer Bennett, Senior Contributing Editor of *Harrowsmith* magazine, gardens in Verona, Ontario. Her most recent book is *Lilies of the Hearth* (Camden House Publishing, 1991).

Clematis 'Ville de Lyon.'

Chapter Three:
Perennial Vines

By Lewis and Nancy Hill

hen the neighbors' children were young, they decided that the tall vine clambering up our porch posts each summer was a "Jack in the Beanstalk" vine because, in their imaginative minds, it seemed to climb up and on forever like the stalk in the fairy tale. Actually, it was the perennial vine *Aristolochia durior*, commonly called Dutchman's pipe, but to them it will always be slightly magical. ∾ Most adults, at least those of us in the Northeast, visualize pink rambling roses covering a Cape Cod cottage when we hear or see the term "perennial vine." And if not roses, then shiny Boston ivy (*Parthenocissus tricuspidata*) climbing massive stone halls of learning or perhaps purple clematis (*Clematis* spp.) drooping over a backyard trellis. These mature vines are engagingly displayed in garden magazines and nursery catalogs in idealized images that make us long for similar plants of our own. ∾ Perennial vines differ from annual vines not only in that they live for years, but also in that most of them become woody after two or three seasons. A few species, like silver lace, or silver fleece, vine (*Polygonum aubertii*), die to the ground each winter in the North, but most simply lose their leaves or, in the case of

Many perennial vines, like Virginia creeper, can provide vivid color in autumn.

beautiful both on the vine and in dried arrangements, as are the seedpods of clematis. In autumn, the foliage of Virginia creeper (*Parthenocissus quinquefolia*) explodes into a glorious, deep red.

It is difficult to argue with the merits of any of these climbers, but too often when gardeners attempt to create vine plantings the end result is somewhat different from what they had envisioned—not anything like the pictures in the books and catalogs. The plants may be spindly and grow unevenly, or they may be winter-killed. Worse yet, many vines that gladden our hearts for the first few years after planting eventually become eyesores or climb out of control over trees and hedges. Thalassa Cruso, in her classic book *Making Things Grow Outdoors* (Knopf, 1971), bemoans the fact that "choking trash vines" had taken over her property before

some, such as the ivies (*Hedera* spp.), produce foliage that stays on the vine throughout the year.

Their longevity gives them many advantages. You don't need to replant perennial vines each year, and they grow larger and more attractive as the years go by. Many produce ornamental foliage that not only looks good but also can be used to screen or camouflage. Some offer a bonus of lovely flowers or berries. Clematis, honeysuckle (*Lonicera* spp.), climbing hydrangea (*Hydrangea anomala petiolaris*), wisteria (*Wisteria* spp.) and rambling roses (*Rosa* var.) are among the most showy flowering types, and silver lace vine and trumpet vine (*Campsis radicans*) also produce nice blooms. In the autumn, the fruits of bittersweet (*Celastrus* spp.), euonymus (*Euonymus* spp.) and porcelain berry (*Ampelopsis brevipedunculata*) are

Oriental bittersweet, Celastrus orbiculatus, *is cultivated primarily for its colorful fruit.*

she purchased it. Wild roses, wild grape, Virginia creeper and Japanese honeysuckle, all fine vines in their proper place, were the culprits.

Choosing the Right Vine

As in choosing a marriage partner, enchantment at first sight does not always guarantee future happiness. Appearance may be deceiving, so even if you fall in love after seeing a particular vine or a somewhat enhanced photograph, get to know the plant's bad points as well as its good ones. Particularly in the North, you'll need to consider whether or not it will thrive in your growing season. One good approach is to check out the perennial vines already growing in your neighborhood and to judge for yourself how successful they are.

Fortunately, a great many vines are perfectly happy where temperatures fall below zero for much of the winter. Still, people who move to the North from warmer areas are often disappointed to find that they must forgo most of their old favorites. Bougainvillea, creeping fig,

An ideal vine for screening, Dutchman's pipe can climb 25 feet in a single season.

Like other trumpet vines, the hybrid 'Madame Galen' prefers full sun and rich soil.

jasmine and madeira must be forgotten. Certain southern vines, like wisteria and honeysuckle, are able to grow in northern gardens, even in sheltered areas of USDA Zone 3, but it is unlikely that they will bloom as splendidly in Minneapolis as they do in Memphis.

Nearly all the climbers that do well in the North are deciduous, although some species that die back above the Mason-Dixon line are evergreen below it. The foliage of the few deciduous vines that retain their leaves in the North during the winter, such as English ivy (*Hedera helix*) and the sweet autumn clematis (*Clematis paniculata*, now *C. maximowicziana*), are likely to brown enough so they could hardly be called green. Clematis and moonseed (*Menispermum canadense*) are woody in warmer parts of the United States and Canada, but they are herbaceous in the colder regions, where they die back to the ground each fall and sprout again from the roots the following spring.

Most perennial vines grow best in spots where they receive sun at least half of every day. Climbing hydrangea is an exception and does well in either sun or shade. Some species, such as bittersweet, do well in either full sun or moderate shade, but most perennial vines, although they will tolerate some shade, are at their best only when they receive a full day of light.

The right location for your vines is important, but it is equally essential to choose the proper species for the purpose you have in mind. Do you want to block out the trash your neighbor never seems to get around to cleaning up? To provide summer shade for a hot front porch? To camouflage an ugly concrete wall? Or simply to enhance your property with a vine-covered fence, arbor or gazebo?

Mature wisteria vines need a strong support and plenty of room to display their blooms.

Some vines have dainty, thin leaves; others are covered with dense, light-blocking foliage. Some grow with the speed of lightning, but a few take many years to develop fully. English ivies grow slowly, perhaps 3 feet a season; but silver lace vine and honeysuckle can travel two or three times that far in the same span of time. Vines such as Dutchman's pipe can fool you, too. They get off to a slow start, but just when you aren't looking, they begin to grow vigorously. More than once we have had to take out handsome, healthy climbers because they overwhelmed their sites and their neighbors, and we could no longer keep them under control.

Support, Training and Culture

Most perennial vines cling by twining or by wrapping tendrils around trellises or wires. A few, including climbing hydrangea and ivies, grab tightly with special little holdfasts. These suction cups weld to stone, brick and concrete and enable the plants to climb. They also adhere to wood, but it is usually not wise to set such vines against wooden buildings or fences; the heavy foliage holds moisture so effectively that it can rot the wood.

Even vines that don't adhere to surfaces, particularly the perennial vines that stay in place year-round, can have a deteriorating effect on wooden buildings, fences, trellises and pergolas, especially where the climate is humid. We have seen not only the clapboards but the wooden sills of a building rot because vines blocked out sunshine and air over a period of years. When you plant a vine near a wood surface, place the support in such a way that there will be an air space between it and the building, particularly if the vine has heavy foliage. This type of support is also easy to tip away from the structure when you need to paint. To avoid

Lonicera heckrottii, *goldflame honeysuckle, is a trailing perennial climber that looks best* *when its woody stems are permitted to ramble freely atop fences and walls.*

frequent replacement, use supports constructed of aluminum or wood that has been treated with a nontoxic preservative.

Most perennial vines need little training since they are naturally inclined to climb. A few of the twining types, like wisteria, benefit from a helping hand to guide them in the right direction when they're getting started. Even those that ascend with ease may have particular needs. Most twiners, for example, prefer to wrap in only one direction, so steer silver vine (*Actinidia polygama*), common moonseed, akebia (*Akebia quinata*) and bittersweet counterclockwise as you look down on them. Honeysuckles, in contrast, twine clockwise. Some, such as rambling roses, do not twine nor do they have either tendrils or holdfasts, and these vines must be tied to supports.

Perennial vines are generous, and a single plant is all that is needed to mask most trellises. When they are to cover a fence or building, we space most perennial vines 5 feet apart. Some slow growers, however, such as English ivy, should be planted as close as a foot apart for faster coverage.

Directly after planting, we like to add a little balanced, liquid fertilizer—fish emulsion is a good choice—to help the vines get off to a quick start. Mature vines that are growing vigorously need to be fed once a year, at most, if the soil is in good condition, and more nutrients will mean more cutting back. Add fertilizer only when growth seems weak or the foliage is not a healthy color. When vines are growing under the eaves of a building, however, nutrients are likely to be washed out during heavy rains, so additional feeding is often necessary.

Fast-growing vines are best controlled by pruning in summer or early fall, since

One of the most popular of all climbing plants, roses are striking, but they require far more *care than most perennial vines, especially in northern gardens.*

pruning when they are dormant encourages rapid regrowth. At the same time, many flowering species set their buds for next year's blooms during the current year. It's crucial to keep the plant's flowering schedule in mind, especially if you are pruning late in the season; otherwise, you may clip off most of the next year's blossoms. A general rule is to prune immediately after flowering, but there are exceptions to this advice.

Propagation of perennial vines is relatively easy. Sometimes you can start new plants by digging offshoots from your own established vine or from those of a willing neighbor. Although you can propagate most vines by grafting, by rooting cuttings or by planting seeds, the easiest method is to layer them. If this is done in early spring, the buried vine will form roots during the summer, and either that fall or the following spring, you can cut the rooted part from the main vine, dig it up and replant it. There are only a few perennial vines, such as clematis, that form clumps and can be divided into several plants in early spring.

Actinidia polygama

(silver vine)

Of Oriental origin, this ornamental vine is a relative of the kiwi. In Japan, both its leaves and fruit are eaten. The silvery,

Cutting the vines back by about a third each fall will encourage flowering the following year. Untroubled by insects or diseases, silver vine and its cousins are good choices when pretty foliage is required.

Akebia quinata

(five-leaf akebia)

This climber, also called chocolate vine and pronounced *ah KEE bee ah*, is a native of eastern Asia. It takes its scientific name, *quinata*, from its compound, semi-evergreen leaves, which consist of five segments. There is only one other akebia species, *A. trifoliata*, which has three- rather than five-lobed leaves.

Although it can twist and twine 40 feet or more and is vigorous enough to crowd out other plantings, five-leaf akebia still is easy to control and looks nice trailing along fences. Clusters of small, fragrant

heart-shaped foliage is decorative, and we've discovered that cats are so attracted to it that they sometimes claw it to shreds. Another species, the variegated *A. kolomikta*, is also attractive to felines—so much so its common name is cat vine. The bower actinidia, or tara vine (*A. arguta*), is a much more vigorous grower and will extend to 50 feet. It has heavy foliage, but neither the flowers nor the fruit are as attractive as those of silver vine. It makes a good screen but needs careful pruning to keep it under control.

Silver vine would probably be planted more extensively if it didn't take so long to twine its way to its maximum height of 15 feet. It has fragrant, white flowers in early spring. Since it is dioecious, male and female flowers are borne on separate plants; one vine of each sex is needed to produce fruit.

All actinidia species like full sun or partial shade, and they thrive in good soil.

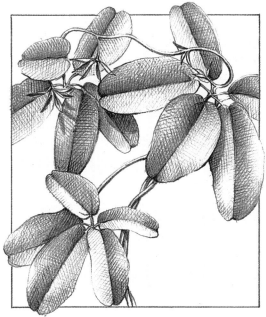

brown-purple flowers appear in spring. If they are pollinated (plants have either male or female blossoms), they produce purple fruits—oddly elongated and edible.

In the South, akebia foliage remains green through the winter months; in northern gardens, the leaves remain on the plants but are browned by the harsher conditions. North or South, akebia vines grow so energetically that you can cut one to the ground in the fall and be guaranteed it will still cover a large trellis the following season.

Ampelopsis brevipedunculata

(porcelain berry)

The porcelain berry, brought from northeast Asia to Europe in the late 1800s, is a vigorous grower with attractive, somewhat open foliage. It is especially suited to low walls that have been trellised, giving the vine's tendrils something to catch, but it also is capable of cloaking large surfaces. A huge old plant has so covered the barn of a midwestern gar-

dener we know, that every time he puts away his tractor he says it's like driving into a bower. A member of the *vitaceae* family, porcelain berry has foliage that looks like that of grapes but turns scarlet in the fall. 'Elegans,' which has green leaves variegated with white and pink, is less vigorous than the species, but is particularly lovely.

It is the fruit, however, not the foliage, for which gardeners cultivate porcelain berry. The berries, held in clusters like grapes, move from yellow-green to glorious hues of blue, shaded with a crackled effect that is exactly like porcelain. No other vine compares with ampelopsis in producing beautiful, colorful fruit.

Once established, the porcelain berry will grow as high as 20 feet. It flourishes in sun or partial shade—an eastern exposure is ideal—is not fussy about soil and requires only a little spring pruning and an annual dose of compost or a balanced fertilizer. Rarely planted or seen, this is a vine with fruit that will make the neighbors sit up and take notice.

Aristolochia durior

(Dutchman's pipe)

Its huge, broad, heart-shaped leaves distinguish Dutchman's pipe, a North American native and a member of the birthwort family, from other vines. That same foliage also makes this vine an excellent choice for screening, and once it was much grown to provide dense summer shade for tall Victorian houses and large country porches. Because it is so vigorous—climbing 20 and 30 feet in a single season—it overwhelms most modern homes and is no longer widely planted.

Its common name comes from its unusual, purple-brown flowers, which are shaped like meerschaum pipes but are not easy to find among the huge leaves. One of the best ways to locate them, ac-

Campsis radicans

(trumpet vine)

Also called trumpet creeper, trumpet flower, trumpet honeysuckle and our favorite, cow-itch, this native vine of North America gamely clings to stone or wood with its aerial rootlets, reaching 30 feet and higher. But its great vigor, its rooting stems and its plentiful seeds mean it can become invasive, so gardeners should think twice before planting it.

Although its compound, toothed leaves are attractive, we grow trumpet vine for its flowers, bright clusters of orange-red, funnel-shaped blossoms that appear in midsummer and last into autumn. They are the favorite of the local ruby-throated hummingbirds as well, and are guaranteed to attract these tiny birds.

cording to a gardener friend, is by their odd, though not altogether unpleasant, odor. But it is for its curtain of leaves, not its flowers, that Dutchman's pipe is cultivated.

Gardeners often become frustrated because the newly set vines tend to grow little in the first few years. But once they are established, they twine skyward so rapidly that they soon become too heavy for lightweight trellises and must be checked. To encourage branching, we pinch the stems in the spring and prune as needed in late winter. If the vine becomes overwhelming, it can be cut to the ground in February, with the surety that it will resprout, vigorous as ever, in spring.

Dutchman's pipe does well in sun or partial shade, puts up with pollution, is immune to most diseases and insects and flourishes in good garden soil amended annually with a balanced fertilizer. This is an antique to be dusted off—a practical, handsome addition to any garden large enough to accommodate it.

Trumpet vines haven't been a focus of modern plant breeding, but there are several cultivars worth considering. 'Flava,' for example, has an all-yellow blossom; 'Madame Galen,' a cross between *C. radicans* and *C. tagliabuana* with pink-orange flowers, is particularly hardy and a good variety for northern gardens; 'Crimson Trumpet' is gloriously true to its name. The species is also choice, however. Garden writer John Sabuco describes an Illinois house, blanketed with *radicans*, as looking like "a huge Sunkist orange."

All cultivars prefer full sun, plenty of moisture and garden soil that drains well. Once trumpet vines are established, they need only to be controlled. Any pruning that is required should take place in early spring, since trumpet vines flower on the current season's growth.

Celastrus spp.

(bittersweet)

Both the Oriental bittersweet, *C. orbiculatus*, and the American species, *C. scandens*, are attractive, vigorous, ornamental vines. (There is also a Korean bittersweet, *C. flagellaris*, which has small berries and thorny stems, but it is not generally available in catalogs or nurseries.) The native *scandens* is more hardy and aggressive than the Oriental form, and it can

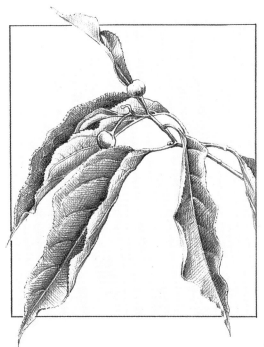

become weedy. Neither species has showy flowers, but the yellow and orange berries of both make bittersweet much prized for fall bouquets and holiday decorations. In the case of the American bittersweet, yellow capsules form on terminal clusters as the flowers fade. These then pop open and the bright orange berries appear. The flowers and berries form in lateral clusters on the Oriental vine.

Bittersweet berries are borne only on female plants, which must be pollinated, so both male and female plants are necessary to produce fruit. One male, however, can fertilize many females if they are growing nearby. Most nurseries now label each bittersweet plant by sex, making it easy to purchase at least one of each gender.

Bittersweets grow well in ordinary soils and in either sun or light shade. They twine beautifully over arbors and other tall supports, but it is not a good idea to allow a bittersweet vine to climb over valuable trees and shrubs. They are so vigorous they shade out their supports, and they can wrap tightly enough around other plants to choke them. In more temperate climates, bittersweet is invasive, but in northern gardens, its aggressive ways can be controlled and its fruit enjoyed.

Clematis spp.

(clematis)

Clematis, which climbs by wrapping its leaf stems, or petioles, around wire, twine or any other slender support, is one of our favorite vines. Although you'll hear it pronounced both *cle-MAT-is* and *CLEM-a-tis*, dictionaries list the latter as correct. However you say the name, the flowers attract attention whenever they are in bloom. And if you choose the proper varieties, that can be for most of the spring and summer. About 50 of the 200 members of the genus are native Americans, but most of the large-flowering cultivars we cherish are complex hybrids of European and Asian species.

Horticulturists divide the large-flowering clematis varieties into three main classes: Florida, or spring-flowering, Patens and Jackmanii. Each group has different flowering habits, which northern gardeners, especially, should understand if they are to grow clematis successfully. Plants of the Florida group bloom during the summer on wood that grew the previous summer. The Patens vines also flower on old wood, but bloom earlier in the season. Those in the Jackmanii group flower on vines that grow the same season. Their blooms appear during the summer and continue until frost.

Gardeners in Zone 5 can grow most of the Florida and Patens hybrids with little trouble. In Zone 3 and all but the most sheltered spots of Zone 4, however, gardeners may need to give members of these groups winter protection by removing the vines from their trellises in the fall, laying them on the ground and covering them, just as with climbing roses. Clematis experts are now reassessing the hardiness of many species and cultivars, discovering *C. viticella* and many others are far more rugged than was previously believed. Before you exclude a particular plant, try to get up-to-date information.

We who garden where winters are severe are safest planting clematis that bloom on new wood—varieties from the Jackmanii group. They can be treated much as we treat our herbaceous perennials. In late fall, after the leaves turn brown, we cut the plant down to about a foot above the soil surface. The following spring, the new sprouts that come from the roots grow so rapidly that they easily recover their trellis, even if it's a good-sized one. Jackmanii varieties run into the hundreds and bare-root plants travel well, so gardeners should take advantage of specialized firms like Steffen's and not

settle for the one or two varieties that are available locally.

Not all clematis have large blossoms. The sweet autumn clematis (*C. paniculata/C. maximowicziana*), a species from Japan, China and Korea, is a fast-growing, semi-evergreen vine with beautiful dense foliage and tiny, wonderfully fragrant, white flowers. These are followed by silvery seed clusters that last long into the fall. Like Jackmanii types, the sweet autumn clematis should be cut back severely in late winter. It is considered hardy only to Zone 5, but we grew one for several years in Zone 3 in a sheltered spot. We finally took it out because it bloomed so late in the season that its flowers nearly always were caught by our early frosts. Yet another Vermont gardener, only 30 miles south of us, has blossoms every year.

Sweet autumn clematis is only one of many smaller-flowered types—or species with atypical blooms—that are hardy in northern gardens. Although they are less easy to find in nurseries and catalogs, *C. alpina*, *C. macropetala*, *C. ligusticifolia*, *C. recta*, *C. texensis*, *C. tangutica* and *C. serratifolia* are all worth getting to know. They include the only truly yellow clematis and plants with bell-shaped flowers as well as vines with foliage that is entirely different from the oval, leathery leaves typical of more familiar varieties.

Although clematis are not demanding, they have distinct requirements that must be met. Far less fussy than was once believed, they prefer a pH that ranges between 6.0 and 7. The soil should be light and fertile and plant roots should never be allowed to dry out. We cover the roots with a mulch of lawn clippings and water our vines during dry weather. Clematis also like a sunny location, but prefer their roots to remain cool. An ideal placement is a northeastern or eastern exposure. Keep the vines at least 2 feet from brick, stone or concrete walls, because such structures collect heat, which warms and dries out the soil.

Pruning is sometimes necessary. The best time to do this depends upon whether the vine blooms on last year's wood or on the current year's growth. Cut back the vines of the Florida types lightly, and only right after they flower. The Patens group may need heavier pruning, and the recommended time to do it is in early spring before the new growth begins. When pruning the Jackmanii types, climate makes a difference. In locations where the vines winter over and become woody, prune them in early spring, to 2 feet from the ground. In the colder areas, where the vines die back each fall, simply remove the dead vines. When the first sprouts that appear in the spring are about 12 inches tall, we pinch them back to make our vines more bushy.

Few insects bother the clematis. Diseases are not usually a problem either, although almost all gardeners have been or will be visited by the mysterious clematis "wilt." Long thought to be caused by a fungus, clematis wilt may be nothing more than a structural weakness—a failure of the thin stems to carry enough water from the roots to the leaves. Whatever the cause, once plants wilt there is little to be done beyond cutting them back.

Euonymus fortunei

(winter creeper)

Euonymus is used more often as a ground cover than as a climber, although the many available cultivars offer a wide variety of climbing habits and ornamental features. Ascending types are sometimes grouped under the name 'Erecta.' Some kinds, such as 'Carrierei,' cling well to walls; 'Gracilis' offers variegated foliage, as do 'Sunspot,' 'Variegata' and 'Uncinata.' There are also yellow-leaved types and varieties whose green foliage is marked with yellow centers or yellow

edges, as well as cultivars, like 'Minima,' with miniature leaves. Nearly all have attractive red or orange berries, although their flowers are negligible.

Most varieties of winter creeper grow well if set in good soil in a sunny location, although their rambling is subdued when compared with that of silver lace vine or clematis. If you want your plants to climb, you must direct them up the support surface, at least at the beginning of their journey. Interestingly, euonymus is one of those plants whose appearance—leaf size and shape—changes as the vine matures.

It is also one of the few evergreen vines for northern gardens, but without protection from winter sun and wind, even euonymus will brown and die back. Pruning is rarely necessary, but winter creepers are susceptible to scale. Spraying with a dormant oil in early summer is the best prevention.

Hedera helix

(English ivy)

English ivy is the best known of the hederas, both in this country and in temperate Asia and Europe, where, in ancient times, ivy was sacred to the Roman god Bacchus and was believed to be protection against intoxication. Although the species is of marginal hardiness in Zone 4, some of its cultivars are considerably tougher. It is evergreen in sympathetic climates, but in northern gardens tends to brown from sun and wind during the cold months.

English ivy is long lived, but is a slow grower. Once its rootlets take hold, however, it is unsurpassed in its capacity to coat surfaces, especially in shade. It often seems its shiny, leathery green leaves sheathe half the college and university buildings in North America, traveling up their brick and stone walls three stories and more. It is in those settings that mature plants bloom and produce ber-

ries—which are poisonous—but a flowering English ivy in a northern garden is rare.

British colonists carried English ivy to America more than 200 years ago. Today there are scores of cultivars available to gardeners, including the rugged 'Baltica.' 'Bulgaria' and 'Wilson' are two more choices for the cold-climate gardener. The many fancy-leaved types—variegated, ruffled and edged—are, regrettably, too tender to grow successfully in the North. If you plant English ivy, buy the hardiest cultivar you can find. Unfortunately, some of the varietal names have been mixed up, so to be sure of getting a cold-resistant strain, start a plant from a neighbor's vine if you can. English ivy cuttings root quickly in water or moist sand.

Hydrangea anomala petiolaris

(climbing hydrangea)

A native of Japan and China, this vine was imported to America in the 1860s. It produces large, flat clusters of small white flowers and clings tightly to brick, cement, stone or wood by small holdfasts,

often reaching heights of 70 feet. In England, climbing hydrangeas are frequently allowed to climb up the trunks of large trees.

Although the blossom clusters (made up of tiny fertile flowers and larger, 1-inch sterile blooms) are pretty, climbing hydrangeas, unlike their bush cousins (*H. arborescens*), are grown primarily for their foliage—finely toothed, shiny oval leaves that turn a pale gold in the autumn.

This vine does well even on northwest walls, where it gets little light, but it prefers a slightly more sunny site. It may get off to a slow start, but it is vigorous once it is established, good for covering unsightly walls or screening unattractive views. Like most perennial climbers, it benefits from being planted in slightly acid soil, rich in organic matter, and from being fed with a balanced fertilizer each spring. Disease and insects are rarely a problem, and pruning is usually necessary only to maintain shape or size. One of the best of the clinging vines, it is also attractive during the winter, since the woody stems turn a reddish color when the plant is dormant.

Lonicera spp.

(honeysuckle)

Honeysuckle, to most northern gardeners, means a large upright shrub covered with pink or white flowers in the spring and soft, red berries (and robins) in the fall. But in the South, another member of the family has long been praised in song and verse—the fragrant honeysuckle vine. While they can be trellised against walls, these vines look their best when their fast-growing, twining stems are allowed to ramble along walls or over arbors. Above all, they are vines grown for their wealth of flowers, not for their heart-shaped leaves.

A shade-tolerant American cultivar introduced in 1862, Hall's honeysuckle (*L. japonica* 'Halliana') is one of the most widely cultivated varieties. Its highly fragrant white flowers turn yellow in early summer and later produce black fruits. Unfortunately, birds eat and spread the seeds, and it has become a trash vine in some locations. *L. japonica* is native to Asia and is hardy throughout the United States and southern Canada, except for Zones 2 and 3. *L. henryi*, hardy to Zone 4,

is less rampant than Hall's. In colder regions, the native trumpet honeysuckle vine, *L. sempervirens*, whose red and orange flowers are followed by red berries, is a better choice. 'Dropmore Scarlet,' a *L. x brownii* cultivar developed in Manitoba, has bright red flowers—but no fragrance—and thrives even in Zone 2.

Aphids sometimes plague honeysuckles, but otherwise these vines are pest and disease free. While honeysuckles do best in rich garden soil, they are remarkably tolerant of less than ideal conditions, including shade and drought. Plants that have become tangled or overgrown should be pruned, but not until you and the hummingbirds have had an opportunity to drink your fill of nectar from the tube-shaped flowers.

Menispermum canadense

(moonseed)

Moonseed, a native of eastern North America, is a vigorous, fast-growing vine with large, lustrous, ivylike foliage. Its flowers, cup shaped and greenish yellow, are inconspicuous but appear throughout the summer. Although moonseed is sometimes called yellow parilla, its common name comes from the crescent-shaped seed within the toxic black fruit that forms in the fall. It is not a tall grower, but the foliage is dense and attractive, especially when allowed to twine along fences and over walls.

Moonseed has many good points, but it is not a good choice for every purpose. Even though it dies to the ground during the winter in northern areas, it grows back rapidly, and the vine's underground rhizomes produce new plants so vigorously that it can quickly become invasive if not firmly controlled.

On the other hand, moonseed is one of the handful of vines that will thrive in a shady, wet setting and will put up with wind and poor soil. We prune only to

shape, taking care not to drop the cuttings, which root easily. Once out of bounds, moonseed is nearly impossible to rein in.

Parthenocissus quinquefolia

(Virginia creeper)

In the North, Virginia creeper is commonly called woodbine (a name also used for *P. inserta*, which is distinguished from *P. quinquefolia* by its lack of adhesive discs on the tendril tips). This hardy native is great in the right places, but it can become a plague in the wrong ones. It is able to grow in a wide range of conditions, and can shinny up trees, up guy wires on utility poles and along fences, clinging tightly with its tendrils. Planting one is an important decision, since once the vine is established it tends to take over and is difficult to eliminate. When kept firmly in hand by pruning, however, Virginia creeper is attractive and succeeds where other vines fail.

Because it grows so rapidly and to con-

Orient, not the Bay State. It is sometimes called Japanese creeper, or Japanese ivy, and is a relative of Virginia creeper (*P. quinquefolia*), although it resembles English ivy in that its adhesive discs are able to bind to stone and brickwork. Boston ivy is widely planted where English ivy is not hardy, and you'll see it decking out schools and public buildings in the colder regions of North America. Blanketing large, flat surfaces is what it does best. Its shiny green foliage, shaped rather like maple leaves, turns a rich red orange in the fall; Boston ivy flowers, which appear only on old vines, are inconspicuous, but are followed by lustrous, blue-black berries.

This climber grows much faster than English ivy and can quickly reach the top of a 60-foot building. Even when it suffers winter die-back, it regains its tidy good

siderable heights, it is often used for covering unsightly trees, fences and buildings, even piles of junk. Although it is a master at rambling, Virginia creeper also has adhering disks and rootlets as well as tendrils that allow it to scale. In autumn, its compound leaflets—toothed, dull green and bunched in fives—turn bright red. (New growth is also touched with red.) Earlier in the season it produces innocuous flowers that are followed by bluish-black berries, beloved by birds.

Virginia creepers grow well in sun or partial shade and willingly suffer both dry and poor soil. Like other members of the *vitaceae* family, they are popular with Japanese beetles, but overall are resistant to disease and insects. 'Engelmannii,' the only commonly available cultivar, has smaller, less coarse foliage.

Parthenocissus tricuspidata

(Boston ivy)

In spite of its common name, this vine of the grape family is actually from the

looks within weeks. It tolerates shade, dry soil and urban pollution, but prefers sun, enriched soil and good air circulation.

Like several other vine species, as Boston ivy plants mature they have the odd habit of producing differently shaped foliage: single heart-shaped leaves, leaflets in threes and large, three-lobed leaves.

Numerous named varieties have been introduced, some with smaller, more attractive leaves, such as 'Lowii,' which has foliage that is deeply cut and crinkled. 'Veitchii' turns purple in the autumn, rather than red; 'Robusta,' according to some catalogs, is particularly hardy. Most cultivars, however, are not as vigorous as the species.

Polygonum aubertii

(silver lace vine)

This native of Tibet and China is also called China fleece vine and silver fleece vine. And lace flower and mile-a-minute vine. One of the most vigorous of the perennial vines, it can twine with stem and tendril to a height of 25 feet or more in a single season. It has attractive light green

foliage that becomes shiny as the season passes, and in late summer and early fall, the vine is covered with foamy, 5-inch clusters of small, fragrant, white flowers, reminiscent of autumn clematis. Its late-blooming habit, flowering when many garden plants have gone by, makes it especially valuable, but its vigorous growth is sometimes a problem when you're trying to keep it under control in a small garden.

Discovered by a French missionary, Georges Aubert, silver lace vine is a member of the buckwheat family. It does well in sun or partial shade and asks for little more than rich, well-drained soil. It is unbothered by wind and pollution and will survive even if killed back during winter. Many northern gardeners, in fact, cut their plants to the ground in late winter.

While silver lace vine is willing to climb, it is at its best when it is allowed to sprawl and tumble and wander along the tops of walls and fences. Prima facie evidence of the excellence of the species is the fact that not a single *P. aubertii* cultivar is available from a North American nursery.

Rosa spp.

(climbing roses)

With the exception of some seaside dwellings, the rose-covered cottage of the storybooks is not common in the frigid regions of the United States or Canada. And for good reason: climbing roses are not reliably hardy in the colder zones. If they are to survive, you must remove the canes from the trellis and cover them each autumn. That chore, frankly, is more than most gardeners care to undertake. Moreover, since the long canes of climbing roses do not twine, or have tendrils or holdfasts, you must guide them up a trellis or other support and fasten them. Finally, the thorny canes must be pruned regularly. In a nutshell, climbing roses in northern gardens are real work.

mail-order companies specializing in older varieties have them. Good, too, are climbers bred by Wilhelm Kordes, such as the crimson-red 'Dortmund,' which are recognized as a class under the name *kordesii*.

If protection against the cold of winter weren't challenge enough, climbing roses are heir to all the diseases and insects that plague other roses. Northern gardeners enlisting in the rosarian army need to think twice—even three times—and then seek specific advice from one of the many good books dealing with the culture of this demanding genus. Only the serious and committed should enlist, but those who grow roses successfully insist these climbers are worth all the trouble.

Wisteria spp.

(wisteria)

Wisterias are able to twine upward to a height of more than 20 feet, although they can be pruned to grow into a bushy shrub. In addition to the native species and those that have been imported from the Orient, there are dozens of named varieties that produce pink, bluish violet, reddish violet, pink or white blooms, some of which are fragrant, as well as a considerable collection of hybrids. Most varieties bloom in May and June, producing stunning displays with their pendulous clusters of flowers.

Wisterias vary widely in hardiness, and although we usually think of them as suitable only for a southern bower, some will grow in sheltered spots even in Zone 4. Unfortunately, the flower buds are extremely tender, easily nipped by a late frost. One gardener near us, in Zone 3, grew a husky wisteria on her barn for more than 10 years, but it never produced a single bloom.

Wisterias are long lived, but many plants start slowly and take several years before they blossom. To avoid the wait, try

But there are the rewards of spectacular blossoms and fragrance, the traditional gifts of roses. The list of the many climbing and/or rambling cultivars includes trailing sports of numerous tea roses as well as hybrids of such species as *R. multiflora*, *R. wichuraiana* and *R. setigera*. Some flower for much of the summer, while others bloom only once for a period of two or three weeks. Among the disease-free cultivars most hardy are 'John Cabot,' a double pink-red, and 'William Baffin,' with flowers the color of strawberry ice cream. A promising new variety is 'Aïcha,' a large-flowered yellow.

Gardeners in Zones 3 and 4 may get good results from choosing older roses, such as 'Red Excelsa' and 'Pink Excelsa,' which are exceptionally hardy and need only to be laid on the ground for winter protection. Unlike many of the new cultivars, these heirlooms are not grafted, so should they die to the ground, the new shoots that come from the roots are like the original. Unfortunately, they are not readily available at local nurseries, but to find potted vines that have already flowered. It is also important to buy wisteria from a nursery that propagates its plants by grafting, layering or taking cuttings, because vines grown from seeds or offshoots may take a decade to bloom. Always prune off any suckers coming from the roots of grafted wisterias, since these new plants will be inferior but are likely to grow so rapidly that they crowd out the grafted part of the plant.

Wisterias also sometimes fail to bloom if they are growing too vigorously (often the result of too much nitrogen in the soil). To prevent this, gardeners slow the growth by cutting back vines in late spring, or they root prune the vines heavily in early spring. The addition of a fertilizer high in phosphorus, like bonemeal, also can stimulate blooming, especially when combined with root pruning. Flower buds for the following year are formed early in the summer; keep this characteristic in mind when pruning the vines.

Japanese wisteria, *W. floribunda*, is considered slightly more hardy than Chinese wisteria, *W. sinensis*; it is also more fragrant. And in one of those odd quirks of nature, Japanese wisteria twines from right to left, Chinese from left to right. 'Alba' (white), 'Rosea' (pink), 'Longissima' (lavender) and a rare double-flowered purple, 'Violacea Plena,' are four Japanese types worth trying where conditions are favorable.

Because there is wide variation in hardiness among the many cultivars, purchase plants grown by a nearby nursery or in a climate similar to yours. Moreover, wisterias are not easy to transplant, so buy plants in pots, not bare-root vines, and grow them in a spot where you aren't likely to need to move them later.

Wisterias like protection from the wind and they prefer full sun and good garden soil, rich in organic material. When vines have covered the area reserved for them, pinch back side shoots to encourage the growth of flower-bearing spurs. Prune out old wood as necessary when the plant is dormant, and allow new wood to replace it. If you are growing a variety that is not grafted, you can renew it by cutting it back nearly to the ground.

A building smothered with wisteria is a magnificent sight in the springtime. These are also excellent vines for arbors and pergolas—anywhere they can create green roofs—and for climbing trees, but the structure should be at least 10 feet tall to allow the racemes to hang freely and really show off.

Lewis and Nancy Hill live in Vermont's Northeast Kingdom, where they operate a nursery, Vermont Daylilies. Their most recent book is *Daylilies* (Storey Communications, 1991).

Common allamanda, Allamanda cathartica.

Chapter Four:
Indoor Vines

By Tovah Martin

bout fifty years ago, flowering vines were planted to wander over the walkways in our greenhouses. It was a revolutionary move at that time, especially in a commercial greenhouse. But eventually the vines became part of the scenery, shading the valuable undergrowth against the blazing summer sun and setting the mood under glass. ◁ Rumor has it that Uncle Ernest Logee was responsible for putting in the first vine. While his competitors were busy simplifying their commercial glass houses into sparse and naked concrete edifices, Uncle Ernest was transforming his crystal kingdom into a jungle of groping vines. He dug down deep beneath the midbeds, slipping the plants out of their pots and into the ground underfoot, letting the roots sink directly into good New England soil. Several years passed while the vines plunged their roots downward and simultaneously snaked slowly up their supports to reach the greenhouse summit. Several more years elapsed before their groping hands stretched out to join fingers and pleach overhead. ◁ In the midst of all this progress, other family members were busy navigating hoses and manipulating spray rigs around the fledgling vines,

The showy, two-toned blossom of glory bower, Clerodendrum thomsoniae, *consists of orna-* *mental, paperlike white bracts which surround the smaller red flower.*

all the while clandestinely scratching their heads and swearing that Uncle Ernest had gone daft. But when the vines, a decade after they were planted, began to transform our greenhouse into the indoor Giverny that Uncle Ernest had envisioned, our attitudes toward him were transformed as well. Now we can scarcely imagine the greenhouse without its tunnel of verdure. Before we realized it, adding new creepers whenever space permitted had become a family tradition.

Actually, the vines provide much more than mere greenery. Even during the winter, when the vines are pruned back to bare bones, they carry a smattering of blossoms. In summer, when they are allowed to intertwine unhindered, the golden trumpet vines (*Allamanda cathartica*), bougainvilleas (*Bougainvillea* spp.) and glory-bowers (*Clerodendrum thomsoniae*) dominate the scene, stealing the show from the small plants on the benches. Those wandering vines with their roving branches and eye-riveting blossoms have transformed a commercial greenhouse into an indoor garden, which is precisely what Uncle Ernest had in mind all along.

In Praise of Indoor Vines

One glimpse of these blossom-bright climbers proclaims their aesthetic virtues beyond doubt. Vines sell themselves. What's more, vines are more visible in the greenhouse than in the garden outside; they take on a larger persona indoors. Wisteria (*Wisteria* spp.) wandering around a wall outdoors provides a poetic backdrop, but a bougainvillea showering blooms from the peak of a greenhouse roof steals the scene.

Vines give you something gorgeous to

look at, and they also camouflage the girders and sash bars that you would rather not see. Nothing dissipates the illusion of a lush indoor park as rapidly as the framework of a greenhouse. Metal support poles and heating pipes are infinitely unpoetic; foundation masonry hits the eye as a discordant element under glass. Part of the beauty of vines indoors is their ability to obliterate the skeleton of a greenhouse, or a window, and flesh it out in an appropriately botanical way.

But vines put forth more than just another pretty face. They earn their keep indoors. Prior to the arrival of the vines, our glass roofs were painted with shading to prevent the begonias within from burning under the intensity of the strengthening sun. Beginning in mid-spring, Uncle Richard Logee, never known for his gracefulness, had to climb the fragile roof of the greenhouse, balance himself on the slender sash bars and paint a mixture of hydrated lime, casein and water on the panes, knowing all the while that the shading would become progressively diluted with each ensuing thunderstorm. In a few weeks, he was up there again, repainting the glass.

Today you can purchase premixed shading compound that is applied only once a season or you can install blinds or netting to shade a greenhouse. But none of those solutions imparts a garden ambience to the plants below. A fairly densely foliated vine, on the other hand, provides a dappled screen between the sun and the greenhouse benches. Even a windowsill, a window greenhouse or a sunroom can benefit from the natural curtains provided by climbing plants. And as an additional bonus, shade vines also lower the indoor temperature by as much as 20 degrees F on sizzling summer days. They cut the blaring sun and double as living fans when the incoming breezes touch their broad foliage. The resident tropicals rarely complain when the thermometer

hits 130 degrees F, but the incumbent gardeners tend to melt. The vines make life bearable.

Vine Requirements

Vines seemed like the logical choice for a family like mine, one more comfortable wielding trowels than paintbrushes. But make no mistake: vines are not maintenance-free. First of all, they require a network of supports—either sturdy lathes for the heavier climbers such as allamanda or bougainvillea to lean on, or wires aloft for dainty vines such as grape ivy (*Cissus rhombifolia*) and passionflowers (*Passiflora* spp.) to navigate. You needn't worry about the aesthetic value of these frameworks. Before long, the vines will do an excellent job of screening their supports from view.

Tender vines, like this bougainvillea, can both shade and beautify a greenhouse.

As with any plant, insect control, feeding, grooming and pruning must be accomplished regularly. Nothing is more hideous to the eye than a bower of brown leaves hanging limply overhead. And there are few sights as ravishing as a neatly manicured arch of blossoms gracefully enveloping a greenhouse, small or large. Vines can set the stage or ruin the

Sun-loving Mandevilla x amabilis *'Alice du Pont' is a vigorous climber.*

performance, depending upon their upkeep.

Before you choose an indoor vine entirely on the basis of its stunning good looks, there are several practical considerations to ponder. Keep foremost in mind the light requirements of the crop growing below. If you have sun-worshipers such as pelargoniums, cacti, succulents or herbs growing underneath, shade vines become a liability rather than an asset. If you have plants like impatiens or begonias, species that prefer dappled shade, choose vines such as allamanda, jasmine and cissus that will form partial screens. If you are growing shade-demanding foliage plants such as ferns below, you can safely plant a dense covering vine such as passionflower, Carolina jessamine (*Gelsemium sempervirens*) or blue clock vine (*Thunbergia grandiflora*). Always consider the needs of botanical

residents dwelling below before placing a vine in a greenhouse.

There's no reason a vine must provide permanent shade, however. Although the planting will remain intact throughout the seasons, vines can be manicured according to your whims and needs. Most vines can be pruned heavily in winter to allow light to penetrate during the dark days of the year, and then their roving branches can be encouraged to grow out again to form a protective bower in spring. But keep in mind that a stern haircut just before flowering season will curtail the performance of winter bloomers such as Carolina jessamine and winter jasmine (*Jasminum polyanthum*).

There's also the issue of invasiveness to consider. Certain vines, such as creeping fig (*Ficus pumila*) and grape ivy, can be a handful unless you prune continually. They provide a wonderful cover-up for an unsightly wall, but they move like kudzu to encase whatever falls in their path. By all means, use creeping fig and ivy to your best advantage, but let these aggressive vines loose only in situations where they won't become the resident botanical bullies.

Planting Vines Indoors

The vine-planting process indoors is not dramatically different from the procedures followed to establish vinery outside. Indoor vines are planted in exactly the same way that you slip vines into the garden. If you prefer to keep the root system safely confined to a container, use a large pot—it's nearly impossible to transplant an established vine once it has begun wandering. If you prefer to place the vine directly into the ground, you'll enjoy faster growth and be saddled with far less care.

A sturdy support is required to hasten the upwardly mobile stem. For that purpose, we enlist the same metal poles that

The brightly flowered, fast-growing Bengal clock vine, Thunbergia grandiflora, *gets its common name from its habit of twining clockwise as it ascends its support.*

support the greenhouse benches, encouraging the vines to act as camouflage for the existing edifice without cluttering the scene with additional unsightly posts and beams. Painted metal is much more satisfactory than wood, which eventually disintegrates. And plastic just doesn't synchronize with the mood, even for the brief amount of time when it is exposed. But there is a gray area: the original support, remember, will soon disappear behind the vine.

There are all sorts of vines out there—tendril graspers, twiners and leaners—and all should be tied to their supports initially. Even self-propelled vines such as star jasmines (*Trachelospermum* spp.) should be tied securely to supports in their formative stages, and many vines such as bougainvilleas and passionflowers must be guided throughout their careers. It's far better to coax a vine gently toward your preferred course before it has made a contrary decision of its own.

Once the vines have climbed to the upper story, the pleaching process begins. We string heavy wires horizontally a foot apart several yards above the benches in need of a canopy. As soon as the first branches hit the horizontal supports, they are headed gently in that general direction to form a green roof. Because leaves will scorch if they touch the glass, we leave a good 2-foot buffer zone between the arbor and the top of the greenhouse. For heavier vines, such as bougainvillea and allamanda, we use dowels or thin lathes laid horizontally between two poles as an

57

Passionflowers, like this fragrant South American native Passiflora vitifolia, *are easy to culti-* *vate and make excellent indoor plants. They climb by grasping with tendrils.*

Despite its name, Madagascar jasmine is a stephanotis, *not a true jasmine. Its waxy, white* *flowers are fragrant, opening in late spring and lasting throughout the summer.*

underpinning for the vines. Initially, the vines finger their way along the supports and form a sparse lacework of branches. But with time and pruning, the stems branch out until they've formed a thick mass with plenty of foliage and an abundance of blossoms.

The Care of Indoor Vines

Gardening is an ongoing affair, and indoor vine cultivation is certainly no exception. Pruning and grooming are our most time-consuming chores. We prune our vines back dramatically in autumn, when the days visibly begin to shorten, and we repeat the pruning process in mid-winter if the overhead cover becomes too dense. When pruning in the fall, we're careful not to cut back winter-blooming species such as passionflower or vines that produce their flower buds on old wood, such as glory-bower and its cousins.

Even during the summer, when a vine's services are most in demand, there's no reason not to thin the branches to allow more light to penetrate. When you prune, try to remove all those clinging tendrils that are wound around the wires. They might look like cute little curlicues while green, but they're destined to turn brown and unsightly after a few weeks' time. We also cut out branches that swoop too low and remove arms that are headed toward the glass, since their foliage will scorch the minute it hits the panes.

Grooming is a major chore with a dense cover of vines. Even a fastidious vine will have a few yellow and brown leaves or spent flowers grasped in its roaming arms. Rather than trying to penetrate the overgrowth with clippers, take the vine and give it a good, stern shake. Most of the debris will fall in a shower that can be raked from the walkways below.

Our in-ground vines require much less work than their potted neighbors. When planted directly in the soil, climbers dry out half as frequently as their potted compatriots. They rarely show signs of starvation, but nonetheless, they should be fertilized with any balanced food at least once a month during their growing season.

Insect control can pose a perturbing problem with indoor vines. The dense mass of foliage is a perfect haven for all sorts of pests. The best weapon is vigilance—check the foliage regularly for aphids, red spider mites, whiteflies and mealy bugs, then nip the infestation in its bud. (Fortunately, beneficial insects can also have a field day in the foliage of vines growing in a greenhouse.) Because insect control is cumbersome with vines, you may want to avoid growing species that are especially prone to attack. Among the most problematic are the many members of the legume family, which attract red spiders, and plants from the verbena and nightshade families, beloved by

The marbled leaves of bougainvillea 'Harrisii' provide additional visual interest.

whiteflies.

In spring, when our greenhouse is filled with delicate flowers swaying overhead and the glass resonates with the hum of appreciative honeybees, the demands of vines seem small. Every year a song sparrow builds her nest aloft and flits among the blossoms and foliage. Leaves intertwine, tendrils grasp their supports and blossoms spill earthward. Such sights and smells never come out of a paint can, as Uncle Ernest knew.

Allamanda cathartica 'Williamsii'

(golden trumpet vine)

Imagine a few dozen 5-inch, blaringly bright yellow trumpets suspended rather precariously from a network of brittle woody branches and you've conjured up

Many climbers, like grape ivy, Cissus rhombifolia, *can be grown successfully in containers.*

a fairly accurate vision of 'Williamsii,' my favorite allamanda. There's no missing this robust vine—it focuses all attention upward. Not only are those trumpets big,

broad and colorful, they also emit a wonderful wine fragrance that spills from their throats only after dark.

Allamanda is a buxom leaner with thick, woody stems surrounded by whorls of deep green, 4-inch leaves. Give the stem a sturdy support and coax it upward by lashing it to the guide. Then, when your plant reaches canopy height, begin pruning to encourage branching and use crosshatched lathes overhead to hold the weighty growth.

Vines produce a smattering of flowers all year, but blooms are most prolific in summer. To encourage maximum output, give plants full sun and feed them once a month. Pests rarely bother allamanda's thick, waxy foliage, but cold

temperatures—less than 60 degrees F at night—will set back these natives of the South American tropics. To make a long blooming season possible, be sure to allow the plant to rest for several months during the winter by keeping the soil nearly dry and withholding fertilizer.

Bougainvillea spp.

(bougainvillea hybrids)

There's nothing like a cloud of colorful bougainvillea blossoms to transform a greenhouse into a botanical paradise. It seems that Uncle Ernest had some inkling of that fact, for he began his canopy-planting escapade with bougainvilleas, and those same multi-hued vines still form an overhead lacework in our greenhouse.

These natives of the tropics are often likened to sweet peas, and there is some resemblance between paper-thin sweet

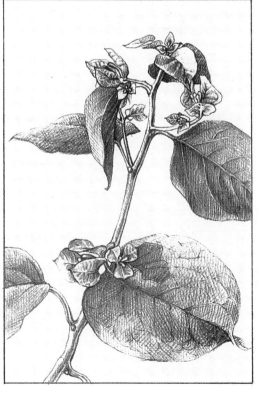

pea petals and the equally brilliant shades of diaphanous bougainvillea flowers. But no sweet pea ever tarried for the amount of time that a bougainvillea remains in blossom, and no legume ever put on such an exotic show.

Bougainvilleas boast an extremely broad color range, including crimson, pink, orange, salmon, yellow, lilac and white. The true flowers are invariably white and inconspicuous—it's those showy blossom-encasing bracts, or modified leaves, that sport all the different shades. The ornamental bracts appear throughout the year, although plants can slip into a resting period if temperatures dip below 60 degrees F in winter.

Bougainvilleas wilt easily, but the foliage will perk up as soon as water is given. In fact, I've discovered that a slight wilt encourages profuse blossoming. We fertilize bougainvilleas once a month, from spring until fall, then withhold fertilizer during the winter months.

Since bougainvilleas are twiners, they require a sturdy support not only at the beginning, but throughout their journey. Although the stems become woody, they resprout willingly after winter pruning.

Cissus rhombifolia

(grape ivy)

Not all vines produce blossoms, and in some situations, a dense tapestry of foliage can be just as pleasing as bright flowers. If you have a shady wall to cover, grape ivy may be the perfect vine. Its foliage is reminiscent of grape leaves, but it also reminds me of another climber, poison ivy. A second look reveals the leaves are shinier, denser and smaller. And nontoxic—you can fondle cissus to your heart's content without suffering any aftereffects.

Grape ivy is a tendril climber that ascends in a delightfully independent fashion. Before you know it, it accomplishes its mission, whether it is acting as a botanical cover-up or a green canopy. It

is bothered by few pests—occasionally visited by mealy bugs and scale—and rarely wilts or requires grooming. Pruning is necessary, however, to keep this climber from covering the world. Aside from that one chore, grape ivy is a blissfully easy living screen.

Clerodendrum thomsoniae

(glory-bower)

Not all vines want to sprawl horizontally. The glory-bower, for example, prefers to take a vertical stance. Throughout spring, summer and early autumn, the broad, shiny, deep green leaves form a backdrop to display the plant's showy blossoms. Like the bougainvillea, ornamental bracts are part of the show—in this case, they are white and look like inflated balloons. The bracts alone would be ample entertainment, but then come the actual flowers, pushing their deep scarlet petals from the midst of the pure white

Ficus pumila

(creeping fig)

The creeping fig immediately comes to mind when the subject of invasive climbers is raised. We have discovered *F. pumila* roaming from the greenhouse into poorly lit offices and onward into the pitch-black cellar. If we look the other way for more than a week or two, we find it cheerfully taking over, obliterating benches, walls, glass and other plants. There are times when we curse the day the creeping fig was introduced into the greenhouse, yet if something needs to be camouflaged hastily and completely, no vine does a better job.

Like cissus, creeping fig is a foliage vine. It is related to the edible fig, but rarely sets fruit. This is a heavy-duty vine by anyone's standards: the dense, deep green, oval leaves enshroud their victim completely, and the sucker roots that sprout along the stem enable it to settle in wherever a snippet lands. When we prune and a tiny segment falls by the

bracts. The whole costume bears a resemblance to bleeding heart (indeed, the plant is sometimes called bleeding heart vine), but its growth habit is vastly different.

Give the glory-bower a strong support on which to twine, then begin pinching back stems while the plant is young to encourage broad as well as tall growth. If you're aiming to cover a wall, use wires running vertically to start progress in the right direction and tie the vines to their guides as they travel.

This vine prefers warm temperatures, 70 degrees F during the day and not below 60 degrees at night. It will endure cooler climates but slips into dormancy in a chill. The broad, hairy foliage will wilt if it isn't watered frequently, and whiteflies can be a pressing problem. But the stunning blossoms—which should be removed when they are spent—compensate for every bit of care the vine demands.

wayside, we can be certain to find a nice green fig blanket spread over that spot in a month's time.

If you can deal with its pugnacity, the creeping fig is easy to grow. It doesn't seem to require any care; coddling merely encourages its wayward ways. Creeping fig needs water once in a while, but our vines wander whether we water them or not. They are not prone to insects and demand no food. This is the ultimate cover-up, adept at concealing structural travesties and capable of rendering your indoors a jungle. Or at least a garden. And isn't that what indoor plants are all about?

Gelsemium sempervirens

(Carolina jessamine/Carolina jasmine)

Not only does the Carolina jessamine share a fragrance similar to that of true jasmine, it also has the same affinity for

chilly temperatures. Like *Jasminum polyanthum*, Carolina jessamine stubbornly refuses to set its golden buds

unless the nighttime temperatures dip down to 50 degrees F. The thermometer can climb as high as you wish during the day, as long as the nights are brisk.

As the name implies, Carolina jessamine is native to the southern U.S., where it can be found loitering on nearly every street corner; it is the state flower of South Carolina. Despite such popularity, this belle has a drawback: all parts of the plant, including the sweet nectar of its trumpetlike flowers, are poisonous. The toxicity may be one reason the vine is rarely bothered by insects.

Carolina jessamine is primarily a leaner, although it will do some half-hearted twining. After you initially tie the stems to their supports at every 2 feet, additional basal shoots will take the hint and weave their way upward, the comely, shiny leaves creating a dense mass which covers eyesores rapidly. If you give gelsemium full sun and an autumn of cool nights, and if you water it moderately, the reward is a winter filled with fragrant, bright yellow blooms.

Hoya spp.

(wax plant)

Long before our greenhouse was built, gardeners were busy coaxing hoyas to meander around window frames, to send their sparsely foliated stems twining around cool porches or into the recesses of poorly lit parlors. In those days, hoyas were grown primarily for their wandering foliage: *H. carnosa*, the most common species both then and now, rarely blossoms.

These vines don't demand the humidity and bright light available in a greenhouse. In fact, they'll grow quite nicely in almost any poorly lit, moderately humid location. Heat is rarely a factor either, for hoyas endure temperatures that slip down to 50 degrees F or even lower. And the leathery leaves are rarely visited by in-

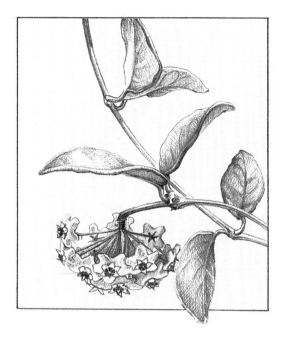

this vine that "blooms in the dead of winter."

In our cool greenhouse, winter jasmine bursts into an intensely aromatic cloud of pure white stars just in time for Valentine's Day. To encourage that show, we keep the house at a teeth-chattering 45 degrees F at night throughout late autumn and winter and work in gloves and wool scarves for the benefit of the winter jasmine vine and its fellow cold-lovers, plants such as acacias, cymbidiums and camellias.

The fact is, you'll never see blossoms on winter jasmine unless you chill it below 50 degrees F for at least four weeks in autumn, and the vine will tolerate tem-

sects except for an occasional attack by scale.

Once in a blue moon, *H. carnosa* produces pinkish-white flowers with red centers, symmetrical clusters of blossoms so waxy they look as if they might be made of plastic. But other hoyas are more prolific. *H. australis, H. carnosa* 'Latifolia' and *H. purpurea-fusca* are frequently bedecked with umbels of star-shaped flowers. They aren't the world's gaudiest blooms, yet there's something intriguing about the hoya's star-within-a-star structure. Perhaps best of all, there are hoyas of all sizes, including a condensed version, *H. carnosa* 'Compacta,' available to accomplish all types of vining missions.

Jasminum polyanthum

(winter jasmine)

Of all the tropical vines in this chapter, the winter-blooming jasmine has received the most publicity. Turn the pages of any horticultural magazine in late fall, and you'll find *J. polyanthum* portrayed in full-colored splendor. The nursery industry has made millions touting the virtues of

peratures as low as 20 degrees if chilled gradually. Winter jasmine will grow lushly in a toasty 80-degree apartment, but it won't flower; buds only set in a chill.

This vine is extremely athletic in any

season, winding its lacy-leaved stems up any foothold to form a thick mass. A post-bloom pruning in spring will keep winter jasmine in check, and indirect sun is sufficient to keep the foliage green. Water jasmine moderately, and feed it once a month with a balanced fertilizer. Other than its autumnal eccentricities, it is easy to please, and its snowy, fragrant blossoms are well worth the cooling that makes them possible.

Mandevilla x amabilis 'Alice du Pont'

(mandevilla)

Mandevilla moves swiftly to achieve its wonders. In a flash, this sun-lover sends its twining appendages straight to the summit of its support. In the meantime, the deeply textured leaves make haste to form a canopy overhead. The coverage is convenient for those of us who need

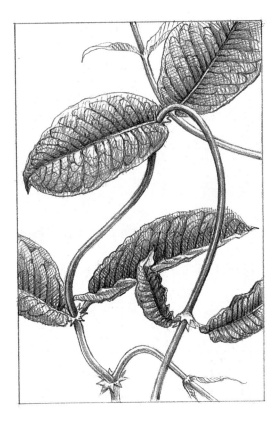

shade, but the main attraction is the plant's profuse, 4-inch tubular blossoms, colored in varying shades of pink and looking very like morning glories. Those soft, satin blooms unfold most abundantly in midsummer and are followed by a smattering of flowers in early winter. Even during the depths of winter, when few blossoms unfurl, the deeply pleated foliage is a handsome sight.

Mandevilla, sometimes known by an older name, *Dipladenia*, is easily cared for. It requires temperatures that remain above 65 degrees F and moderate humidity—though humidity is generally ample for any tropical in a greenhouse environment. The brittle foliage rarely wilts, and the vine invariably appears immaculately manicured. Adding to its virtues, mandevilla is blissfully free of pests and impervious to diseases.

Manettia inflata

(twining firecracker/Brazilian firecracker)

Not all vines are capable of covering a wall in a single season or shading a greenhouse in a few brief years. More modest and compact vines are still valuable to tackle less ambitious projects and to use on windowsills. The twining firecracker doesn't encase everything within reach, and yet its fingernail-sized foliage and slender stems can camouflage a limited area, supplying a small-scale splash of color as well. A leaner, manettia needs assistance as it travels upward.

In fall, inch-long, waxy blossoms smother the plant in a small explosion of firecrackers—or a confetti of candy corn, for the slender, tubular blossoms are bright orange tipped in electric yellow. However, nobody will ever accuse this tropical South American native of being the easiest plant on earth to grow. Manettia can slip into a sulk in late summer, and it's not always easy to nurse it through the pouting period.

caerulea, white passionflower; or red passionflower, *P. vitifolia*. These species bloom reliably, profusely and easily indoors. And what bizarre blossoms they are—like lotus flowers hung in midair, the blooms reach 4 inches in diameter, each boasting a colorful reproductive stalk arising from a crown of filaments against a backdrop of five broad petals and five broad sepals. Passionflowers produce some of the most intricate blossoms known, and a few varieties are fragrant as well.

Water passionflowers when their broad leaves wilt slightly—which is generally a daily occurrence in summer. Plants grow vigorously from January until autumn. It's good to feed this rampant climber generously every three weeks of its active season and to keep a vigilant eye out for red spider mites and whiteflies—they have an affinity for passionflowers, as will anyone who grows them.

The symptoms include browning leaves followed by browning stems and general malaise. The cure is to reduce watering, increase humidity and keep the vine well groomed—one bad patch can spread until the problem reaches epidemic proportions. Full sun is crucial at any time of year, and bright light discourages the onset of the manettia malaise.

Passiflora spp.

(passionflower)

Passionflowers, some of which are American natives, rank among the world's most energetic climbers, hoisting themselves by tendrils that twine around anything within reach. Although the vine itself is featherweight, the combined bulk of the foliar mass requires strong supports. We put passionflowers on the side walls of our greenhouse, where their dense coverage won't completely mask the sun. The vines happily endure partial shade, but the flower buds burst open only in full sun.

Any passionflower will form a foliage canopy. If it's blossoms you want, plant *P. caerulea*, blue passionflower; *P. x alato-*

Stephanotis floribunda

(Madagascar jasmine)

Stephanotis opens its pearly white umbels, or flower clusters, in June—you can set your watch by it. After a winter in

which the svelte, pencil-thick branches twine around everything within reach, clusters of buds begin to swell in spring. The bud stage is long and dramatic, adding to the intrigue until the tubular white blossoms unfold amid the thick, deep green leaves. The climax is a leisurely affair. Once the waxy blossoms open, they last throughout the summer, perfuming the air with their deep-throated aroma.

The thick, almost succulent foliage of stephanotis is visited by few pests and rarely wilts, even if you are negligent with the hose now and then. However, the Madagascar jasmine (which is this vine's common name, although stephanotis is actually not even remotely related to jasmines) does demand warm temperatures. Don't let the thermometer dip lower than 60 degrees F.

Sun is also essential for producing blossoms, but the most important requisite is patience—the Madagascar jasmine may twine several years before it begins blooming. Once the first flowers appear, however, the display will return dependably every June forever after, for the species is famed for its longevity.

Thunbergia grandiflora

(Bengal clock vine)

By some strange quirk of nature, vining members of the thunbergia family invariably ascend their supports by twining clockwise, earning members of that clan the clock vine nickname. *T. grandiflora* is among the most energetic of the genus, sending thick stems and long, broad leaves to strangle supports as it travels

toward the top of the glass. But the fleet-footed acrobatics are only part of the show. In summer, this climber from India is covered with 3- and 4-inch powder blue blossoms. They account for the plant's other common names, skyflower, sky vine and blue sky. (There is also a white cultivar, 'Alba.')

Like other kindred tropicals, Bengal clock vine prefers warm temperatures, 65 to 75 degrees F during the day, 10 degrees cooler at night, and bright sun to produce its heavenly hued blossoms. The clusters of flowers are most profuse in summer, but a smattering of color flecks the vine throughout the seasons. The foliage wilts frequently, demanding constant visits from the hose; however, few insects pester the foliage.

Trachelospermum jasminoides, T. asiaticum

(star jasmines)

Although flowering vines bearing huge, gaudy blossoms visually knock your socks off, they typically provide minimal olfactory entertainment. If it's fragrance you desire, you usually must try a bloomer of more modest dimensions. Each tiny white blossom of star jasmine, *T. jasminoides*, for example, is not particularly eye riveting, although the mass effect of a blizzard of snow white against the deep green vine is lovely. But each blossom emits a sweet perfume, described by Helen VanPelt Wilson as an entrancing cross of jasmine and mock orange.

Vines such as bougainvillea and allamanda form a dappled canopy above the benches in our greenhouse, but the star jasmines weave a tight, dense cloud, neatly camouflaging a singularly unbeautiful pipe network. We tie their leaning branches loosely to the supports just to maintain some semblance of control, but most of their climbing is accomplished in

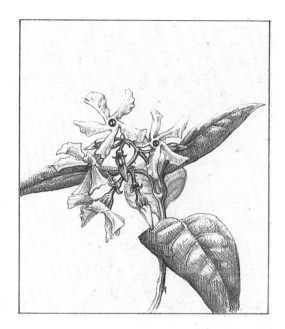

an extremely independent manner with minimal help from the support.

Jasminoides, with its chorus of white, pinwheel-shaped blossoms, is by far the most popular species and is known as Confederate star jasmine in the South. But I prefer yellow star jasmine, *T. asiaticum*, with its eggshell-yellow blossoms and wafting cinnamon perfume. It is a smaller vine with a more modest stature, but a bigger voice aromatically. During the day, the scent is discrete, but it gains body at dusk and intensifies into a heady brew as darkness settles in.

Both are easy to grow. Although sun increases the floral show, star jasmines will blossom cheerfully in partial shade. Their thick foliage rarely wilts, and the plants resist disease and insects. After they've finished flowering, the tidy blossoms wither into oblivion rather than littering the undergrowth, a characteristic shared by far too few other plants.

Tovah Martin, staff horticulturist of Logee's Greenhouses, is the author of *The Essence of Paradise: Fragrant Plants for Indoor Gardens* (Little, Brown).

'Cardinal' table grapes.

Chapter Five:
Edible Vines

By Paul Dunphy

ne of the curious ironies of horticulture lies in its indirectness. As gardeners, we lavish attention on so much of what, ultimately, we don't want in order to obtain the little we do. Willingly we care for an eggplant or water a patch of corn, but only in the hope of coaxing a few purple fruits from beneath the prickly leaves or a few ears from the tall, rustling stalks. With vines, that disparity between the responsibility and the return is especially apparent. ❧ Almost 60 years ago, a gardening authority named Norman Taylor categorized vines as "woody or herbaceous plants that creep, climb or trail." A more dynamic, realistic and only slightly facetious definition would employ action words: vines are plants that bound, engulf or ramble imperialistically. Indeed, the rampant growth of many vines can seem well out of proportion to the harvest. ❧ Like certain pets, vines take a consistent, even-handed discipline before their remarkable versatility can be appreciated. With careful tending, a vine can be one of the stars of the landscape. An arbor of grapes (*Vitis* spp.), say, or maypop (*Passiflora incarnata*) or hardy kiwi (*Actinidia arguta*) can provide it all. The leaves offer shade and color; the

Small squashes can be grown easily, either on wire or net trellises or on fences.

wall-like growth gives definition to a landscape; flowers please the eye. And as the season advances, an edible vine's potential culminates with the ripening of its fruit. Given their promise, food-bearing vines are worth getting to know.

Vines that produce food can be roughly divided into two broad categories: "edible landscape" types, meaning plants that contribute both to the appearance of a property and to the table, and vines that are commonly part of the vegetable garden only. No finality is intended in this grouping. And the possibilities extend far beyond the list that accompanies this section to include such esoteric landscape plants as chocolate vine (*Akebia quinata*), with its tapioca-flavored fruit, or such garden crops as yard long beans (*Vigna unguiculata* spp. *sesquipedalis*) and the nutritious groundnut (*Apios americana*).

In fact, any number of plants have within them a vining potential that can be accentuated by artful pruning. The shaping of landscape plants finds its most extreme expression in what is called espalier, in which any plant, but most commonly a fruit tree, is trained flat against a trellis rather than allowed to grow in three dimensions. Espalier encompasses many techniques and intriguing geometric patterns from simple vertical leaders to elaborate fan and candelabra shapes, fashioned from the outgrowing branches of trees planted only a few feet apart. Proper pruning stimulates the development of fruit-producing spurs and trellising improves the light exposure for each fruit. If an orchardist can commit the time and acquire the pruning skills, espalier can be a magical, living art form that returns a generous harvest from a small amount of space.

Edible Vines in the Landscape

Each edible landscape vine is unique in appearance, growth habit, flavor and site and soil preferences. At the same time, vines exhibit a number of common characteristics and some generalizations can be reasonably applied. All the landscape-type edible vines that follow, for example, are perennials; they should thrive for many seasons. Vineyards planted more than 100 years ago in New York and California are still being tended. Grapes and actinidias have woody stems while others, such as hop (*Humulus lupulus*) and maypop (*Passiflora incarnata*), are herbaceous. Their stems are green and soft and die back in the fall, but in spring, new stems emerge from the soil to bear foliage and fruit.

There is a range in the tolerance to cold of the various vines. All of them benefit from some coddling when they are young. In general, maypop is the most sensitive to cold and *Actinidia kolomikta*, super-hardy kiwi, the most rugged. However, with some protection, such as mulching or a sheltered location, all can endure winter temperatures of at least -10 degrees F and return with vigorous growth in the spring.

With the exception of the super-hardy kiwi, which seems most at home in a slightly shaded location, each enjoys unfurling its leaves in full summer sun, and

Common hops, Humulus lupulus, *is a fast-growing, aggressive vine, able to blanket large* *areas in a single season. Its vines die back in fall in northern gardens.*

all except grapes favor extending their roots into light, well-drained soil with a pH between 6.0 and 6.5. Grapes, too, need a well-drained soil (a high water table can deprive any plant's roots of oxygen), but are most productive in a more acid soil, one with a pH of about 5.5.

The most obvious characteristic of vines is their proclivity to climb. Hop and maypop can extend their tendriled shoots 20 feet or more in a single season. The growth of grapes and kiwis is less explosive but more persistent, for their woody stems do not die back. Growth begins in the spring where it ended in the fall. Actinidias in their native forest regions of northern China, Siberia and Korea clamber up trees to heights of 90 feet or more. In parts of North America, anyone walking through the woods can see wild grapes reaching toward the tops of the tallest oaks and maples.

In a cultivated setting, the growth of edible vines is curtailed and the strength of the plant is directed toward fruiting. The vines are trained to a trellis, the design of which is likely to be shaped by your expectations for the plant. If fruit production is of primary concern, the trellis may be more austere and the training more rigorous than if you are looking first for ornament or shade.

For fruiting, a utilitarian trellis can be constructed of pipe (1½ inch inside diameter) or rot-resistant wood posts (4 inches on a side, standing about 6 feet above ground and connected with 10- or 12-gauge wire). Depending on the training style, the posts may be in the form of Ts with wire strung between them in the fashion of utility lines. Or the trellis can be composed simply of vertical posts joined by horizontal strands of wire.

Where shade or decoration is paramount, edible vines can be trained to a graceful arbor or pergola to provide an arched entrance for a garden or walkway or a green cover for a deck or patio.

Emphasizing screening allows a more laissez-faire approach to pruning, but encouraging herbaceous growth usually means a sacrifice in the quality and quantity of the fruit.

Many mail-order nurseries sell their perennial vines as bare-rooted transplants, that is, with no dirt around the roots. In this condition, the plants should be handled only when they are dormant, commonly in the spring. Some nurseries market vines in containers, and these can be planted at almost any time from spring through late summer as long as the plants have several weeks to establish their roots before the arrival of freezing weather. Like most other plants, vining edibles experience less shock if they are set out on a cool, moist day. A hole deep enough to accommodate the roots, wide enough to allow another 5 or 6 inches of lateral growth and filled with dark, humus-rich soil will give the plant a good start in its new location. Attentive watering further

An old favorite, 'Waltham Butternut' is one of the outstanding varieties of winter squash.

eases the transition from nursery to backyard.

When considering food-bearing perennial vines, keep in mind a caveat of gardening: it is easier to buy than it is to plant. Buoyed up by the pride of acquisition and early-season enthusiasm, I've also learned there is a correlate: it is easier to plant than to provide extended care. So start with only a few vines. Take time to learn at a comfortable pace—not only about the plants but about yourself. Anyone can enjoy eating sweet, juicy grapes in the warm September sun. But before jumping with both feet into a vineyard, discover whether you have the time for pruning and training and whether you enjoy the process. With the inclination and with increased skill, the care of vining edibles in the landscape becomes both simpler and more rewarding.

Cucumbers that are grown on trellises produce straighter fruit and larger crops.

Pole, scarlet and Dutch runner beans, which climb by twining their stems, can be grown on poles arranged like tepees or on strings, wires, fencing or netting.

Vines in the Vegetable Garden

In the vegetable garden, vine crops present a curious set of opposites in terms of space and seasonal requirements. To paraphrase the familiar nursery rhyme:

Some like it hot,
Some like it cold.
Some like it on the ground
And some on a pole.

What these vines have in common, however, is of greater significance than their differences. Their output is both diverse and delicious, from the first tender peas of June to the sweet melons of late summer and the granddaddy squashes of fall.

Garden vines may be broadly classed as either climbers or ramblers. The appropriateness of each type is, alas, tied to the size of one's vegetable patch. Hardly any garden is too small for pole or scarlet runner beans (*Phaseolus vulgaris, P. coccineus*), which can readily twine themselves around stakes on the perimeter of the garden. Peas (*Pisum* spp.) and Chinese yams (*Dioscorea batatas*) can also exploit vertical space and are conveniently accommodated on a garden fence. Climbers make a small garden seem large.

Ramblers, on the other hand, force many people to confront the limitations of their gardens. The space demanded by pumpkins (*Cucurbita pepo*) or squash (*Lagenaria siceraria, Cucurbita* spp.) or melons (*Citrullus lonatus, Cucumis melo* var.) can necessitate hard choices when there is room for only a vine or two. One pumpkin, after all, will easily blanket 40 square feet. And trying to train a pumpkin or large squash to a trellis is, if not impossible, impractical. The fruits are so heavy that each one must rest in its own sturdy hammock.

Vegetable breeders have sought to curtail the imperialistic habit of many vines by turning them into docile bushes. Seed catalogs now offer bush cucumbers, bush squash, even bush melons and pumpkins.

Although they are climbing plants, pumpkins are typically too large to trellis. They belong to the cucurbita *genus, which also includes winter squash and gourds.*

Space has been saved, but flavor has been lost. Relatively flavorless crops such as cucumber and zucchini may prosper on a bush, but large squash and most melons cannot acquire a sweet, complex taste without a generous canopy of foliage to gather sunlight and convert it into food energy and sugars. Big fruits and vegetables require big vines.

The effort to accommodate ramblers led me to broaden my boundaries, even my definition of "garden." I plant cucurbits on the edge of my perennial bed, for example, and let them trail onto the lawn. Another innovation I like is to use landscape-sized "pots" to grow vine crops. I fashion a ring of wire fence 3 feet tall and roughly 2 feet in diameter, fill it with old leaves and top it with 8 or 10 inches of compost and soil. A vine crop planted on this "hill" can trail down the side of the container and across the lawn. I mow the grass until the vines become too long and sinewy to move without damaging them—then leave them to compete with the grass. The arrangement is not ideal, for cucurbits prefer a weed-free (or, in this case, grass-free) environment, but if the option is a small harvest or no harvest, almost any innovation appears attractive.

Vegetable vines span the growing season. In my western Massachusetts garden, peas can be planted early in spring, about the same time as onions. They are tolerant of late frosts and averse to the hot, humid conditions of summer. Most other edible vines are sensitive to frost and cannot be safely planted until the ground is warm. At the same time, many of these crops, particularly melons, require weeks to mature. Caught between the danger of spring frosts and the demand for a long season, northern gardeners must start most vining vegetables and fruits indoors, about a month before it's safe to set tender plants outdoors.

Bringing vines like melons to fruiting challenges gardeners to influence conditions that are beyond absolute control. They must exploit science to achieve horticultural art. The use of grow lights can aid in starting seedlings. Plastic mulch can heat the soil. Lightweight row covers can warm plants and fend off insects in

Grown as an ornamental, scarlet runner beans, Phaseolus coccineus, *have small, flaming-* *red flowers that are followed by long green pods* *filled with mottled pink-purple seeds.*

the early stages of plant growth. Combined, the techniques create a more beneficial environment than insensitive nature would provide. Yet the results of all the climatic manipulation remain in doubt until the moment the orange flesh of 'Flyer' or 'Savor' is sampled.

Gardening is never a surefire proposition—"a thing that rots if you water it and dies if you don't," the anonymous definition of a garden goes. Seed packets and seedlings come with limited guarantees. Some of the food-bearing vines that follow are enigmatic—prospering for several seasons and then disappearing without a trace—some are nearly foolproof and many are challenging. But all can be rewarding. Growing a few of them will add a new direction, indeed, a new dimension to your garden.

Actinidia arguta, A. kolomikta

(hardy kiwi)

While the fruit of a hardy kiwi is smaller than the familiar fuzzy kiwi found in supermarkets (*A. deliciosa*), its flesh is an equally deep, radiant emerald green. Sweeter and with smoother skin, it can be eaten whole like a grape. As with the fuzzy fruit, the flavor of the hardy kiwi approaches that inimitable blend of pineapple and strawberry, with an occasional suggestion of mint.

Curiously, hardy kiwis were widely planted earlier in this century on estates and campuses, strictly as ornamentals. Actinidia foliage is attractive, particularly that of the mature male *A. kolomikta*, which in early summer is beautifully variegated in tones of light red, pink and deep green when situated in full sun. And tucked beneath those colorful leaves are white flowers that give way, in pollinated female plants, to clusters of fruit that ripen from mid-August to late September, depending on the variety.

For fruit production, *A. arguta* has certain advantages. Its fruit is larger than that of kolomikta and, unlike kolomikta fruit, does not tend to drop as it approaches ripeness. A mature arguta vine may bear 75 to 100 pounds of fruit. Varieties such as 'Meader,' an American cultivar, and 'Ananasnaja Michurina' are hardy to about −20 degrees F and require at least 150 frost-free days to mature fruit. 'Issai' is slightly less cold tolerant but is self-fertile. Other kiwis normally require male pollinators.

Productivity aside, the kolomikta, known both as super-hardy kiwi and arctic beauty kiwi, is more decorative and less rampant and demands considerably less pruning than argutas. Kolomiktas can endure severe cold, roughly to −40 degrees F, and need 130 frost-free days to produce ripe fruit. 'Krupnopladnaya' and 'Pavlovskaya,' both bred in the Soviet Union, are among the most productive, largest-fruiting cultivars.

Although tolerant to extreme cold, hardy kiwis can be killed by fluctuating winter warm spells followed by deep freezes. In late fall, many growers wrap the trunks, especially of young plants, with burlap or a special white, corrugated plastic. Another requirement for fruitful cultivation is well-drained soil; damp ground is a frequent cause of the debilitating fungus crown rot. Like most vines, actinidias are more productive if trained to a trellis. Since plants flower and fruit on new wood, most pruning is done in late winter, while the vines are dormant.

Citrullus lanatus

(watermelon)

As delightful a passage as ever has been written on watermelons occurs in Forrest Carter's *The Education of Little Tree*. A wide-eyed, warm-spirited boy embodies the impatience of many a gardener, anxious for that moment of ripeness but frustrated by an inability to tell when the moment arrives. "When you are certain that the watermelons are ripe," Little Tree sagely advises, "they're not."

Contemporary plant breeders have tried to simplify the divinations by introducing varieties like 'Golden Midget' and 'Golden Crown.' Both are relatively early, pink-fleshed melons with skin that signals ripeness by turning from green to yellow-gold when the fruit is ready. No thumping here.

Northern gardeners will have trouble ripening large, green-skinned melons such as the oblong classic 'Charleston Gray,' but the smaller, round varieties— 'Garden Baby,' 'Sugar Baby,' 'Jade Star' and 'New Hampshire Midget' among them—may well achieve perfection. The best oblong watermelon for cold areas is 'Sweet Favorite,' which produces 10-pound fruits covered by striped skin. Seedless types, such as the recently introduced 'Jack of Hearts,' have obvious

appeal, but require a seeded variety nearby for pollination. Oblong, round or seedless, watermelons must be begun indoors. Once outdoors, they demand sweet soil (a pH above 6.0), plenty of moisture until the fruits are set and full sun. Most gardeners in the North use black plastic mulch and row covers to help create the warmth watermelons need.

To confirm ripeness, look for two signs in addition to administering the traditional thump: when the melon is mature, the portion of the fruit that rests on the soil typically turns yellow and the tendril closest to the watermelon stem dies.

Cucumis melo var.

(melons)

Thoughts of picking moist, sweet melons motivate northern gardeners the way the hand of the princess inspired the young heroes in fairy tales: imagining the prize blurs the mind to the rigors of winning. Success in both endeavors seems to require not only a thoughtful strategy but also a touch of luck—or magic. Melons, probably like princesses, are a demanding lot. They want heat but not humidity. They need plenty of moisture, but they wilt with overwatering. Mildew can shrivel the leaves; beetles can bring bacteria. And the growing season always

seems a week too short.

The orange-fleshed, grapefruit-sized Charentais group of melons, varieties like 'Prior' and 'Flyer,' have the best chance of achieving ripeness in northern settings. Also good for colder gardens are the rough-skinned, orange-fleshed cantaloupes 'Gaylia,' 'Minnesota Midget' and 'Early Dawn.' Other frequently recommended varieties for cool climates are 'Earligold,' 'Sweet 'n Early' and 'Sweet Granite.' Green-fleshed honeydew types are more problematic, being larger and slower to mature, but 'Rocky Sweet' and 'Earli-Dew' are among the most precocious.

The best hope for a melon harvest lies in setting out hearty transplants about the first week of June, or when both the soil and nighttime temperatures have warmed. Seeds can be sown indoors in April or early May in containers that are 1 inch in diameter for each week the plant will be inside.

Meanwhile, scoop out and mix with compost an area in the garden about 2 feet wide and 1 foot deep as a "hill" for each two or three plants. Add enough compost to raise the hill 4 inches from the surrounding soil and make a shallow depression to catch water. Then, to raise the soil temperature, cover the hill and the surrounding soil with plastic mulch—either black plastic or the new infrared-transmitting plastic, which allows more warmth to reach the ground but still blocks the light that would encourage weeds. Once the danger of frost is past, cut a hole in the plastic and set the transplants.

Shrouding the plants with a lightweight row cover will add warmth and ward off cucumber beetles, carriers of bacterial wilt. But when female flowers begin to open, remember to remove the cover to allow the bees to do their work. To concentrate the plant's energy, I pinch off late blossoms that won't have time to develop.

Because of the large size of the fruit, melon vines are allowed to ramble, not encouraged to climb. When the vines trail off the plastic, put a board or shingle under the developing melons to keep them off the soil. Wait to harvest until a light tug breaks the fruit from the vine or until the blossom end of the melon is soft and the melon is rich with the aroma of ripeness. Patience is a virtue, for unlike an apple, a melon will not sweeten off the vine.

Cucumis sativus

(cucumber)

The popularity of cucumbers in home gardens has dipped in the past 30 years, as gardens have become smaller and people have devoted less time to pickling and canning. Too bad, because plant breeders have been busy all the while, instilling cukes with greater insect and disease resistance, a milder flavor and greater productivity, even making them "burpless."

The path to a cucumber revival may include these cautious steps. First, try some of the newer varieties, slicing or salad cultivars such as 'Marketmore 80,' 'Hybrid Burpless' or 'Slice Master,' or one of the smaller pickling types like 'Conquest,' 'Calypso' or 'Gerkin.' Or try one of the "Beit Alpha" salad cucumbers from Israel, such as 'Saria,' which are meant to be picked when they are only 6 inches long, or one of the slender French varieties like 'Vert de Massy.' Second, to avoid overproduction, set out only a few plants, 8 to 10 inches apart in a row, or two or three plants to a hill. And third, if space is limited, train the plants to poles or a trellis.

Cucumbers are willing climbers,

although they do not twine themselves around a stake as a pole bean does. On a pole, they must be guided and tied. A better support is a trellis, which their tendrils can grab; the central runner can be grown to the top, then pinched to encourage lateral growth. Vining cucumbers generally produce greater yields over a longer time than bush varieties, and trellised plants produce more fruit than those allowed to ramble. Finally, pick cucumbers young, before the seeds develop and the flesh acquires any bitterness.

Natives of India, cucumbers thrive in a long, warm season. Temperatures in the mid-40s can damage the vines, setting back their growth for weeks. For an early harvest, the seeds should be started indoors in 2-inch containers. Once the soil has warmed and all danger of frost is past, the plants can be set outside. Within eight weeks you can begin to enjoy the cucumber's revivifying coolness, an ancient antidote to the enervating heat of summer.

Cucurbita moschata, C. maxima, C. pepo

(winter squash)

The deep orange flesh of winter squash seems both fact and symbol of the fall harvest. Started indoors and transplanted after the danger of frost has passed, winter squash are picked before the first below-freezing temperatures blacken the vines. The hard-shelled fruits can be cured in the field for about a week—covered each night to protect them from frost—then stored in low humidity at temperatures in the 50s. They will keep for many weeks, rewarding the gardener, meal after meal, for a summer's labor.

Botanists have divided winter squash into three species: *C. moschata, C. pepo* and *C. maxima*. Moschatas are characterized by hard, slender stems that flare out where they attach to the fruits. The

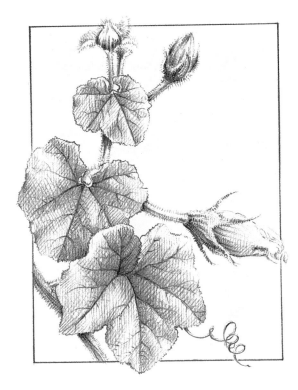

green, blocky 'Buttercup' and 'Chestnut,' a 2-pound variety with sweet, dry flesh.

Cucurbita pepo

(pumpkin)

As the season progresses, pumpkins seem to develop personalities as much as a botanical ripeness. Their odd shapes and varied sizes endow them with more character than any other vegetable. Even the names of some of the new varieties—'Ghost Rider,' 'Spirit,' 'Big Moon'—suggest an anthropomorphic presence, not just a vegetable, emerging from the pumpkin patch.

Slow to mature, the largest varieties, such as Howard Dill's prize-winning 'Atlantic Giant,' can take more than 3½ months to reach full size; smaller types, like 'Jack Be Little' or 'Munchkin,' require only a few weeks less. Like winter squash, pumpkins will not overripen; they can be left on the vine until a cool night wilts the leaves. And like squash,

relatively dense stems afford some protection from the ravages of squash vine borers, gray-white grubs that work through stems, wilting vines and spoiling gardeners' harvest dreams. Among the recommended moschatas are 'Waltham Butternut,' an AAS winner in 1970, and the slightly smaller 'Ponca,' an early butternut type from the University of Nebraska.

Pepo varieties, which have sandpaper-rough stems that are deeply grooved but soft inside, include some of the most flavorful winter squashes, such as 'Delicata,' a long, cream-colored variety striped with green; 'Fordhook Acorn,' a popular older variety; and 'Jersey Golden Acorn,' a 1982 AAS winner. 'Cream of the Crop,' a 1990 AAS winner, has cream-white skin and a mild, nutty flavor. Maximas take in, as the name suggests, the vining giants—'Blue Hubbard,' 'Chicago Warted' and 'Boston Marrow'—as well as a number of 3- to 6-pound fruits such as the teardrop-shaped 'Red Kuri,' the dark they must be protected from frost: freezing damages the shell and hastens decay.

Starting seeds indoors three or four weeks before the frost-free date—in containers with a diameter of at least 4 inches—gives plants a head start on the season and on insect pests. Pumpkins are susceptible to squash bugs and the squash vine borer. A particularly damaging pest, the borer emerges from one of many eggs laid at the base of the plant by an orange and black moth; the larvae then tunnel through vines, causing them to wilt and eventually die. Cutting open the vine and puncturing the borer, then burying the vine and generously watering the plant, offers the only hope for recovery. Where borer damage is known to be high, transplants should be protected with a lightweight row cover when they are set out.

Turning the soil in the fall and rotating crops help reduce borer problems, but strong plants are the best natural protection. I set plants three to a hill with the hills spaced 6 feet apart. Pumpkin vines, among the most rambunctious, can ramble 30 feet and more. The diminutive 'Mini Jack' is a good variety for pies, but is typically grown for its hull-less seeds; 'Trick-or-Treat' is another cultivar with hull-less seeds.

Despite the differences among varieties, all pumpkins are surprisingly similar in taste. Small ones, though, are easier to scoop out and quicker to bake than their larger cousins are. In truth, pumpkin is rarely as smooth as squash in a pumpkin pie, but squash is rarely as attractive as a pumpkin for a jack-o'-lantern.

Dioscorea batatas

(Chinese yam)

Better known as cinnamon vine for its cinnamon-scented white flowers, Chinese yam has quite a surprise in store for gardeners who dig beneath the surface: the tubers of this climbing perennial are as large and tasty as most potatoes. If these tubers did not extend underground to depths of 3 feet, beyond the reach of commercial harvesting equipment, the Chinese yam might rival the potato in culinary and agricultural importance.

Chinese yams can be dug in the fall,

after the vines die back. Tubers left in the ground or replanted in the spring (either whole or in pieces) will generate new growth. Vines can run 10, even 20 feet in a season, but growth is light and not invasive. Plants will be more productive and foliage more lush if the plants are given a support around which they may twine their stem tips.

The Chinese yam is related to an equally fascinating plant called the air potato, or air-potato yam (*D. bulbifera*). Highly cold sensitive, this vine forms edible tubers in the joint between the leaf and stem. Chinese yams, too, develop air potatoes in their leaf axils, but they reach only about the size of a pea. While too small

83

for cooking, these bulbils can be picked and sown to generate new plants.

Because the Chinese yam is late to emerge, northern gardeners will want to extend their season and increase yields by starting plants indoors in pots. Transplanted into the garden after the threat of frost has passed, Chinese yams take hold quickly. Hardy, independent and surprisingly free of disease and insect pests, they approach what many gardeners often long for: potatoes without blight and without the baneful Colorado potato beetle.

Humulus lupulus

(hop)

Although hops are traditionally grown for their pineconelike flower, an ingredient in the brewing of beer, the spring shoots of these willowy vines can be snipped and cooked like asparagus. In fact, pruning 6 or 8 inches from each pencil-thin stem will not only produce an occasional side dish but, as one nursery-

man wryly noted, "it will keep the vine from taking over as quickly as it might otherwise do."

Even in the North, hops are aggressive. Multiple shoots can ramble 20 feet, even more, in a season, and roots will send off new shoots in unpredictable directions. Yet hops are not necessarily overbearing, for the vines are wispy and die back each autumn in cold regions. To keep growth trained to some sort of trellis, prune rigorously at the base of the plant each spring—removing about half the new shoots—and hand guide the twining runners during the summer.

For the landscape gardener, part of the appeal of hops is their rapid growth. The large, light green, fuzzy leaves make this perennial a ready source of shade. One cultivar, 'Aureus,' has yellow-green leaves. There is also a Japanese species, *H. japonicus*, that has bright green foliage and is grown as an annual in the North. 'Variegatus,' as its name suggests, has leaves streaked with white.

All hop plants flourish in full sun and rich, well-watered soil, but they also will endure partial shade, wind and drought—even a busy gardener's benign neglect.

Passiflora incarnata

(maypop)

The hardiest of the more than 250 species in the passionflower family, maypop has piqued the interest of adventurous northern gardeners with both its showy flowers and its vaguely apricot-flavored, gelatinous fruit. Gradually the range of this vigorous perennial has extended as far north as central New England and the upper Midwest.

Unusually late to emerge in the spring—growth is often not apparent until June—the maypop seems to compensate by bursting forth in a bamboolike rush, extending 20 feet or more in a season. By

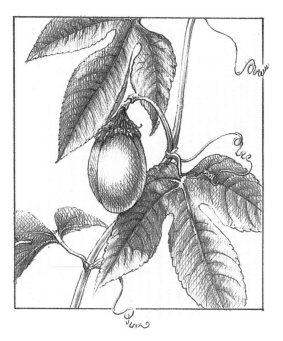

Phaseolus coccineus, P. vulgaris

(scarlet runner and pole beans)

The small, deep red flowers of scarlet runner bean (*P. coccineus*) flash like beacons from the tips of the light green vines, attracting not only pollen-collecting insects but hummingbirds as well. From the fading flowers emerge green pods filled with a half-dozen beans colored pink-purple and mottled with darker tones, like clouds drifting across a late evening sky.

The flowers and foliage combine to merit scarlet runners a decorative role on a porch trellis or garden wall. Planted 6 to 8 inches apart and given a surface to climb, the plants will weave themselves into a dense, foliated quilt, 12, 15, sometimes 20 feet tall. In mild climates, scarlet

July, the 1- and 2-inch flowers are unfolding their lavender or white petals, exposing frilly crowns of purplish pink. Although each flower lasts but a day, new blossoms open throughout the summer.

The number and shape of the flower's parts symbolized the crucifixion to earlier botanists, hence the genus name *passiflora*. The common name maypop, according to some, is derived from the bang emitted by the yellow-green, egg-sized fruits when they are suddenly squeezed. Others claim maypop is an anglicization of an Indian word meaning "rattle fruit," a reference to the sound made when the dry fruits are shaken. This American native's name might just as well have come from the plant's habit of running underground and then popping up unexpectedly, many feet from the main vine. An expert climber, maypop will wrap its tendrils around a trellis or wire fence or any nearby plant. In southern states, their uninhibited ways have rendered maypops a nuisance, but in the North, where vines die back each fall and sometimes disappear altogether, they are still welcome additions to the garden.

runners and their white-flowered sibling, the Dutch runner, are perennials. Northern gardeners must replant each spring, sowing seed 1 inch deep about a week before the last expected frost.

Pole beans (*P. vulgaris*), another climber, are ideal for gardeners with limited space, and many argue that they are more flavorful than bush beans because of their greater leaf area. 'Champagne,' 'Romano,' 'Kentucky Wonder' and the stringless 'Butler' are all reliable varieties, growing as tall as 10 feet, depending on the height of the pole. 'Kentucky Blue,' a 1991 AAS winner bred by Calvin Lamborn, the creator of 'Sugar Snap' peas, is a highly regarded new cross between 'Blue Lake' and 'Kentucky Wonder.'

I plant six seeds around each pole and then thin to the best two or three. With a little guidance from the gardener, the vines will begin twining themselves counterclockwise around the poles, typically set in tepee fashion, and soon will be out of reach of woodchucks and rabbits. But not of small children, who will delight in taking refuge within a bean tepee.

Pisum sativum, P. macrocarpon

(peas)

Edible harbingers of spring, green peas (*P. sativum*) can engender both pity and awe in a gardener. Suited to cool weather, peas are one of the first crops planted after soil temperatures rise into the 40s. But no sooner do the seedlings unfold their fan-shaped leaves than they are deluged with icy spring rains that would set anyone's spine ashiver. Yet within eight weeks, the vines are 3 feet tall and flecked with delicate white flowers that soon give way to slender pods (which should be picked just after the peas begin to swell and before they have completely filled the pod; frequent picking encourages plants to set more pods).

Pea seed can be planted 1 to 2 inches deep, 2 to 3 inches apart (shallower and closer early in the season when seeds are likely to rot in the cool ground), either along a fence or in double rows in the garden. I separate double rows by about 4 inches and install a trellis down the middle before the seeds sprout. Chicken wire, nylon netting or horizontal strands of twine strung at 4-inch intervals all offer adequate holds for the vines' grasping tendrils. Even the semi-leafless, or "self-supporting," peas yield more heavily when helped to climb.

The pea season can be extended by planting at intervals of a week or so, and by planting both early varieties, such as 'Daybreak,' 'Sparkle' or 'Maestro' with late varieties like 'Green Arrow' or 'Wando.' To vary the harvest further, I grow edible pod types (*P. macrocarpon*). Snow

peas, such as 'Oregon Sugar Pod II' and 'Snowflake,' are picked while the pods are small and flat. Sugar snap types, such as the AAS winner 'Sugar Ann' and the first stringless sugar snap, 'Sugar Daddy,' can be eaten, pod and all, even after the peas have begun to swell.

Peas feed the garden as well as the gardener. In concert with soil bacteria, pea plants, like other legumes, gather nitrogen on their roots. When the pea season has passed, cut the vines off at the soil line rather than pull them up, and leave the roots to enrich the ground for the next crop.

Vitis spp.

(grapes)

Over the millennia, cultivated grapes have evolved a preference for south-facing, sunny, open locations with well-drained soil, free of ledge, hardpan or groundwater. Sloping ground and hillsides too steep for row crops have been extensively planted with the deeply rooted vines, but good garden ground also will support grapes. Ideal conditions include gravelly acid loam (pH 5.5), which retains the warmth of the day throughout the night.

Starting a vineyard is a job for early spring, when vines are dormant. One-year-old stock with a thick, healthy root system transplants more easily and often bears fruit as early as two-year-old plants. Each vine should be set in its hole at about the same depth as it grew in the nursery, the roots carefully spread and the soil, mixed with a handful of bonemeal, returned and gently tamped. The spacing between vines should be between 6 and 8 feet.

Pruning is the enigmatic art of viticulture, at least initially, and has many variations. In general, less is more with grapes: vigorous pruning and thinning of grape clusters will likely yield larger, sweeter fruit. Most garden encyclopedias provide detailed instructions about pruning and are worth consulting before you take pruners in hand. A $15 membership in the Minnesota Grape Growers

Association (Box 10605, White Bear Lake, MN 55110) brings not only the annual yearbook and quarterly newsletter, but also a copy of "Growing Grapes in Minnesota," a comprehensive manual for northern gardeners.

Grape breeders have in recent years released a number of more hardy, productive, flavorful varieties, including the red seedless types 'Einset,' 'Canadice' and 'Reliance.' The blue, seeded 'Price' is widely considered to be an improvement on the familiar 'Concord'; 'Beta' and 'Suelter,' two other hardy blue varieties recommended for jelly, juice or the table, are heirlooms, bred by Louis Suelter in central Minnesota late in the nineteenth century.

Whether grown for a patio canopy or for jelly, juice or the table, grapes are an attractive addition to any landscape. Better still, vines that are faithfully tended will provide joy to more than one generation.

Free-lance writer Paul Dunphy gardens in western Massachusetts and is a Senior Contributing Editor of *Harrowsmith Country Life* magazine.

Virginia creeper, Parthenocissus quinquefolia.

Sources:
Mail-Order Directory

Only the most common vines are easy to find for purchase. While mail-order firms often have cultivars that are unavailable locally, few seed companies or nurseries specialize in climbing plants. To locate everything you want, it is usually necessary to shop from more than one catalog.

It is easiest and fastest to order seeds and plants from within one's own country, but some companies are willing to ship across national boundaries. Although seeds can be mailed across borders without difficulty, plant imports to the United States must include an invoice showing the quantity and value of the plants, as well as a document from the Department of Agriculture certifying the plants are disease-free. Imports to Canada must be accompanied by a Permit to Import (available from The Permit Office, Plant Health Division, Agriculture Canada, Ottawa, Ontario K1A 0C6).

Chiltern Seeds
Dept. HA, Bortree Stile
Ulverston, Cumbria
England LA12 7PB
(seeds: annual, edible, indoor, perennial)

Cruickshank's Inc.
1015 Mount Pleasant Rd.
Toronto, ON
Canada M4P 2M1
(plants: perennial)

D. W. Burrell Seed Growers Co.
P.O. Box 150
Rocky Ford, CO 81067
(seeds: melons)

DeGiorgi Seed Company
4816 South 60th Street
Omaha, NE 68117
(seeds: annual, edible, perennial)

Dominion Seed House
115 Guelph Street
Georgetown, ON
Canada L7G 4A2
(seeds, Canada only: annual, edible)

F. W. Schumacher Co.
36 Spring Hill Road
Sandwich, MA 02563-1023
(seeds: perennial)

Forestfarm
990 Tetherow Road
Williams, OR 97544
(plants: indoor, perennial)

The Fragrant Path
P.O. Box 328
Fort Calhoun, NE 68023
(seeds: annual, perennial)

Gardenimport, Inc.
P.O. Box 760
Thornhill, ON
Canada L3T 4A5
(seeds & plants: annual, perennial)

Gilson Gardens
P.O. Box 277
Perry, OH 44081
(plants: perennial)

Glasshouseworks Greenhouses
P.O. Box 97
Steward, OH 45778-0097
(plants: indoor)

Hortico
723 Robson Rd., R.R. 1
Waterdown, ON
Canada L0R 2H0
(plants: perennial)

J. E. Miller Nurseries, Inc.
5060 West Lake Road
Canandaigua, NY 14424
(plants: edible)

J. L. Hudson, Seedsman
P.O. Box 1058
Redwood City, CA 94064
(seeds: annual, edible, indoor, perennial)

Jackson & Perkins
83-A Rose Lane
Medford, OR 97501
(plants: roses)

Kelly Nurseries
P.O. Box 10
Louisiana, MO 63353
(plants: edible, perennial)

Logee's Greenhouses
141 North St.
Danielson, CT 06239
(plants: indoor)

Mellingers Nursery
2310 West South Range Road
North Lima, OH 44452-9731
(plants: edible, indoor, perennial)

Park Seed Company, Inc.
Cokesbury Road
Greenwood, SC 29648
(seeds: annual, edible)

Roses of Yesterday & Today, Inc.
803 Brown's Valley Road
Watsonville, CA 95076-0398
(plants: roses)

Seeds Blum
Idaho City Stage
Boise, ID 83706
(seeds: annual, edible)

Steffen's Nursery
P.O. Box 184
Fairport, NY 14450
(plants: clematis)

Stokes Seeds, Inc.
39 James Street, Box 10

St. Catharines, ON
Canada L2R 6R6
or Box 548
Buffalo, NY 14240
(seeds: annual, edible)

Thompson & Morgan
P.O. Box 1308
Jackson, NJ 08527
(seeds: annual, edible)

Tripple Brook Farm
37 Middle Road
Southampton, MA 01073
(plants: perennial)

W. Atlee Burpee & Co.
Warminster, PA 18974
(seeds & plants: annual, edible, perennial)

Wayside Gardens
1 Garden Lane
Hodges, SC 29695
(plants: perennial)

Woodlanders, Inc.
1128 Colleton Avenue
Aiken, SC 29801
(plants: indoor, perennial)

Index

Photo Credits

Chapter One
p. 6, Margaret Hensel: Positive Images
p. 9, Derek Fell
p. 10, E. R. Degginger, Ph.D.
P. 11, Derek Fell
p. 12, Nance S. Trueworthy
P. 14, Jerry Pavia
p. 15, Cathy Wilkinson Barash
p. 17, Ann Reilly: Photo/Nats

Chapter Two
p. 18, David Cavagnaro
p. 20, Thomas E. Eltzroth
p. 21, Thomas E. Eltzroth
p. 22, Phil Degginger

Chapter Three
p. 32, Thomas E. Eltzroth
p. 34 (left), Joanne Pavia
p. 34 (right), John A. Lynch: Photo/Nats
p. 35 (left), Thomas E. Eltzroth
p. 35 (right), Jerry Howard: Positive Images
p. 36, Priscilla Connell: Photo/Nats
p. 37, Ken Druse
p. 38, H. Abernathy/H. Armstrong Roberts

Chapter Four
p. 52, Derek Fell
p. 54, Charles Marden Fitch
p. 55, Jerry Howard: Positive Images
p. 56, Charles Marden Fitch
p. 57, Charles Marden Fitch
p. 58, Ken Druse
p. 59, Derek Fell
p. 60 (left), Derek Fell
p. 60 (right), Charles Marden Fitch

Chapter Five
p. 70, Chuck O'Rear/H. Armstrong Roberts
p. 72, David M. Stone: Photo/Nats
p. 73, Charles Marden Fitch
p. 74 (left), Ann Reilly: Photo/Nats
p. 74 (right), David Cavagnaro
p. 75, David Newman: Visuals Unlimited
p. 76, Virginia Twinam-Smith: Photo/Nats
p. 77, Walter Chandoha

Sources
p. 88, E. R. Degginger, Ph.D.